The American Religious Experiment:
Piety and Practicality

The American Religious Experiment:

Piety and Practicality

Edited By
Clyde L. Manschreck
and
Barbara Brown Zikmund

Chicago Theological Seminary

Exploration Press

Chicago, Illinois 60637

This volume is one of the publications in the "Studies in Ministry and Parish Life" series published by the Exploration Press of The Chicago Theological Seminary.

BR
515
.A54

Acknowledgment is gratefully made for the assistance given the Church Leaders and Professional Papers Conference, Chicago Theological Seminary, 1976, by the **American Issues Forum: Chicago,** made possible in part through funds from the National Endowment for the Humanities.

203552

Printed in the United States of America

Exploration Press
of
The Chicago Theological Seminary
5757 University Avenue
Chicago, Illinois 60637

ISBN: Cloth: 0-913552-06-2
       Paper: 0-913552-07-0

Library of Congress Catalog Card Number: 76-7199

Contents

Introduction

Few Americans realize that the two hundred years of national life we are celebrating during the "Bicentennial" are only a little more than half of our total cultural and social history. There are at least one hundred and fifty years of American colonial life *before* the revolutionary war. Indeed, the political experiment designed at the constitutional convention in the last part of the eighteenth century is only one of the more recent aspects of the American journey. From the very beginning, however, the American experiment can clearly be labeled "religious." We all know the story of the Pilgrims seeking religious freedom in Holland and finally landing at Plymouth rock. Similar religious motivations appear many different times in later colonization and immigration. This religious experiment is as unique a story as the political one. It is a story that deserves to be examined.

The American religious experiment is a complicated and diverse phenomenon. Perhaps two words in juxtaposition can be used to capture the flavor of American religious life: piety and practicality. Piety and practicality are actually distant cousins of the ancient Greek dichotomies of spirit and body, eternal and temporal, spiritual and physical. In the history of Christianity the spiritual has generally been regarded as more important than the physical, so much so that things of this world have often been denigrated as secondary. Religion has been slurred for its concern with "pie-in-the-sky." The dichotomy of spirit and body has also tended to regard material possessions, sex, and the physical labor needed to keep self and society going as less religious than idealistic values, virginity, and so-called sacred works. Piety and practicality in the American religious experiment are related to this ancient tradition, but are by no means sharply bifurcated. The frontier, the disestablished voluntary churches, the necessity of pluralism, and the processes of democracy have tended to bring them together. Piety was strongly manifested in the holiness, pietistic movements of the nineteenth century, only to be counterbalanced by the practicality of the social gospel in the twentieth. Repeatedly in American life longings for purposes and identities that transcend this world are counterbalanced by vocational involvements in everyday living. Speculation about the destiny of the universe has its counterpart in concern about present human nature.

Long before 1776 these two traditions combined to give shape to the future of religion in America. One was the Calvinist tradition and the other was Rationalism. Calvinism incorporated much of Lutheranism, with the addition of an emphasis on election and sovereignty of God. Combined with the notion that God was to be glorified on earth in the lives of people, Calvinism engendered theories of resistance to abusive authorities that admirably suited the burgeoning nationalisms of Western culture. For this and other reasons, Calvinism rather than Lutheranism became the predominant international form of Protestantism by the end of the sixteenth century. Both the Puritans of Massachusetts and the Anglicans of Virginia were Calvinists. Largely from this tradition came the pious conviction of the early settlers that they had been elected by God to carve out of the wilderness a promised land.

Rationalism incorporated much of the Renaissance and by 1776 had become strong in this country and Europe. It tended to follow the dictates of reason and to concentrate on the earthly affairs of man. It resented authoritarian religious structures inherited from the past and found dramatic expression in the French Revolution. Tom Paine, Benjamin Franklin and Thomas Jefferson represented this tradition at the founding of the United States. The rationalists prided themselves on their universal tenents, but nationalism was a necessary step toward the political realization of their principles. This outlook coalesced with Calvinistic election to produce a kind of providential chosenness, and righteousness for the new nation, often termed the Religion of the Republic.

Not until quite recently has this Religion of the Republic been seriously questioned. Toleration for a pluralism of religious groups prevailed throughout most of our history, even though some groups who believed or acted strangely were eyed suspiciously. Most Americans felt obligated to bear to the rest of the world the enlightenment of democracy and the salvation of the gospel. It seemed to be our manifest destiny. In the twentieth century the two traditions that created the consensus called the Religion of the Republic have come into question. Our goals are no longer clear. Many issues confront us. What have we been elected and chosen for? Is democracy so enlightened and superior? How can our emphasis on individual happiness and wholeness escape subjectivism and relativism? What is reality and truth? Moral guidelines, whether biblical or national, are no longer firm. Science tends to ignore religion, and some theologians have proclaimed the death of God. It is increasingly difficult to know what is right and wrong. So it is that the American synthesis of piety and practicality seems to have crumbled. We are all searching for the strong foundations that uphold freedom, equality, happiness, and security. We are continuing the American religious experiment to discover what kind of a consensus will prevail in the future.

These are but a few of the issues and questions considered in this book. While the various chapters deal with a variety of aspects of religion in America and reflect the diverse experience and perceptions of the authors, together they explore our ongoing tradition of piety and practicality. They provide in-put and raise critical questions concerning virtually all the major religious developments that have ensued in this country. Hopefully they will challenge us all to appreciate our past and build an authentic religious and political stance for the future.

These essays are offered by the faculty of the Chicago Theological Seminary as our contribution to the bicentennial. Obviously as professors in a traditionally Protestant institution our perspective has certain biases. To overcome our limitations and balance our inquiry into the total American religious experiment, this collection includes two guest papers from a Jewish rabbi and a Roman Catholic priest. The papers are grouped under four headings as indicated in the table of contents: Historical Perspectives, Biblical Reflections, Jewish/Catholic Views, and Social Interrelationships. While these headings denote the general areas, readers will find that most of the chapters might justifiably be placed under another heading as well.

The five chapters devoted to historical perspectives deal with new forms that have emerged in the American experiment. American religious life has been characterized by different if not unique forms of religious organization and expression. It is important to understand the ways American religious manifestations and structures have developed in our national history. Separation of church and state remains a principle of much pride in our religious story. In the twentieth century, however, it has become a focus of censure, inasmuch as loyalty to state has tended to displace loyalty to God. We might say that practicality has displaced piety. Given the history of Christianity and the sacrifices of the early Christians who would not accept the sovereignty of the emperor of Rome, and given the Holocaust that excessive loyalty to Hitler and Nazism engendered, such a tendency in this country has caused misgivings, despite the obvious benefits of pluralism and toleration. The five essays consider this tension in various ways. Professor Clyde L. Manschreck considers the problem from a historical perspective. Professor Charles Shelby Rooks depicts the special nature of black religious life in the American experiment and assesses the effects of the treatment of blacks, their African heritage and their aspirations on the development of religious institutions and theology. Professor W. Widick Schroeder discusses the development of the voluntary church in this country and what this has meant for the churches, some of which were definitely not from a tradition of voluntarism. Professor Barbara Brown Zikmund traces the role of women in the development of denominationalism which has been characterized by strong lay participation, particularly that of women, and calls attention to increasing professionalization in the churches which has tended to reduce the laity to subservience. Professor Perry LeFevre takes four religious-ethical leaders who in different periods of our history were concerned with the "simple" life and describes the changes in our religious ethos reflected in their rationales.

The second section on biblical reflections focuses on key issues which continue to fragment the churches. Two essays lift up questions which remain at the center of American church life. In the first of these Professor Robin Scroggs explores the thorny question of biblical authority and depicts how church people have repeatedly struggled with the practical issue of what to believe. The Bible has been the center of an ongoing evangelical-liberal controversy. In different periods arguments have revolved around literalism, Darwinian evolutionary theories, historical and form criticism, hermeneutics and intransigence on several levels. The contemporary situation is discussed with sensitive insight into the basic problem.

In the second chapter of this section Professor Andre Lacocque considers our "civil religion" from a biblical stance. As a European he views the American scene with a degree of objectivity not always possible for native Americans. Versed in the Old Testament and experienced in what happened under Hitler, Professor Lacocque critically assesses this nation's civil religion. He calls on us to condemn the idolatry of national pride and to remember our Jewish-Christian heritage as children of God.

Although our nation began as a predominantly "Protestant people," the mixture was soon infused with persons from the Catholic and Jewish traditions, giving further substance to our religious history as an experiment in diversity. Under the section on Jewish/Catholic views, two prominent scholars from each of those traditions discuss the involvement of Jews and Catholics in our national story. Rabbi Robert J. Marx, a practicing rabbi at Congregation Solel in Highland Park, Ill., and also a highly respected sociologist, pictures the struggles of Jewish immigrants to survive in a culture that was not always supportive. Yet American Jews not only survived but prospered. Their prosperity often brought as many religious tensions as it relieved. Despite official toleration,

American Jews continue to experience confusion over relationships with non-Jews. Secularism, Nazism, and political Zionism are but a few of the areas of tension and confusion considered by Rabbi Marx.

Professor John T. Pawlikowski, OSM, describes the story of Catholics in America as a search for unity and acceptability. Contrary to the beliefs of many Protestants, Catholics are not monolithic in their commitments. Although the Spanish Catholics were the first to explore the great Southwest and establish missions from Florida to California, Spanish Catholicism had little influence on the development of Roman Catholicism in America. Later Roman Catholic immigrants, particularly the Irish, dominated the growth of Roman Catholicism in the United States. Catholics were the single largest religious body in the U.S. by 1860, but not until well into the twentieth century did the Catholics win acceptability in our Protestant society. Within American Catholicism ethnic loyalties have militated against full-scale unity. Anti-intellectualism and the role of blacks, Spanish-Americans, and women pose significant questions for the future direction of Catholicism.

In the final section of the book four chapters fall under the general rubric of social interrelationships. These essays witness to past, present and future possibilities in the life of American churches. The chapter by Professor Victor Obenhaus opens this section with a look at the history of the Social Gospel, its past leaders, their motivating convictions and some of its manifestations today. In the next paper Professor J. Robert Meyners considers the theme of liberation. Professor Meyners notes the "revolutionary" thread that has been part of our biblical and national heritage, and makes some concrete suggestions for "liberating" today's church. Professor Philip A. Anderson discusses church administration and how it relates to the human potential movement. He examines some of the common statements that one hears at almost any church meeting, points out what is behind such statements and how they can affect the church, and then suggests some theological experimenting that is appropriate to our times. In the last chapter Professor Ross Snyder attempts to capture motifs from the past and develop symbols expressive of religious style and leadership in the present. To do this Professor Snyder examines a Pilgrim multiplet to provide a model of the full-orbed leadership that religion continually needs to be viable in our culture.

As with most collections of papers or essays there is an inevitable discontinuity and variety. The American religious experiment, however, lends itself to this format because of its innate diversity. We are hopeful that scholars, clergy and laity will find these pages thought provoking. The book is designed to be used in several ways.

First, at the end of each essay the authors have indicated the sources they have used, and usually included suggested references for further reading. None of these chapters pretends to be comprehensive. We invite our readers to move beyond these pages to explore American piety and practicality on their own.

Second, the editors have prepared a study guide to facilitate group use of this volume. In our bicentennial celebration it is important for church people to think together about some of these issues. Church-state relationships, black religious experience, voluntary organizational life, the role of women and the question of Christian lifestyle remain topics that all of us might explore more deeply. As people nurtured in our faith by the biblical tradition the essays on the evangelical-liberal stance and civil religion may help us clarify our loyalty to the Bible. It is important to remember that the American religious experiment was not exclusively Protestant. The two chapters on Judaism and Roman Catholicism will enrich our awareness of this diversity. And finally, the last section of the book contains essays to spark our thinking about the future. Questions of social activism, liberation, administration and leadership can profitably be approached with one of these essays as a stimulus. We hope that this volume will serve as an introduction for various forms of adult study and discussion in the church. The American religious experiment continues in us.

CLYDE L. MANSCHRECK and BARBARA BROWN ZIKMUND

CHURCH-STATE RELATIONS — A QUESTION OF SOVEREIGNTY

By CLYDE L. MANSCHRECK

Church and state in their interrelatedness stand at the center of religious developments in America. This is true not only for the bicentennial period, 1776-1976, but also for the equally long preceding period when the nations of Europe were vying for colonial empires. By 1776 the face of religion had already changed from what it was when the early Anglicans settled in Virginia and the Puritans in Massachusetts. That both of these major religious group were Calvinistic is often overlooked. An examination of the Thirty-nine Articles of 1563 reveals that Anglicanism was Calvinistic in nature. The Marian exiles, who had fled from Queen Mary a decade earlier and returned to England when Elizabeth I became ruler, had come under the influence of John Calvin during their exile on the Continent. Their views heavily influenced the Thirty-nine Articles. The Puritans were even more radically Calvinistic, for they were Anglicans who felt that the church under Elizabeth had not gone far enough in ridding itself of the "dregs of popery." These two groups with their Calvinistic background largely shaped the early religious ethos along the Atlantic seaboard. While different in polity, they shared a sense of divine mission. Conditions in America especially the frontier, the arrival of other groups with differing religious dogmas and polities, and the rise of rationalistic thought greatly affected that early religious ethos, but Calvinism was there to dominate the beginnings of the American religious experience. A few of the basic elements which derived from Calvinism will be mentioned shortly.

Even earlier than the Anglicans and Puritans were the Spanish explorers who introduced aspects of Spanish Catholicism from Cape Hatteras to San Juan Capistrano. Almost a hundred years before the Virginia and New England Settlements, Hernando Cortez in 1519 led a band of conquistadors from Cuba to Mexico. Within a very short time they captured Mexico City and made Montezuma a prisoner, for the Aztecs believed that Cortez was their ancient white god Quetzalcoatl returning. Using Mexico as a base, missionaries, particularly Franciscans, ac-

1

companied expeditions into the vast expanses of the Southwest in search of gold and souls. Coronado roamed over Texas, Colorado, Oklahoma and New Mexico. Others scouted California. Still other Spanish explorers made settlements in Florida. Ponce de Leon explored that region in 1521; De Soto discovered the Mississippi in 1541. On this vast area Spanish Catholicism left its imprint, especially in California and the Southwest where thousands of Indians were converted and religious compounds built, many of which are still operating today.

The French also brought Catholic missionaries with them when Cartier, Marquette, and La Salle explored territories bordering on the St. Lawrence River, the Great Lakes, and the Mississippi. In the 1600s they established a line of scattered forts and missions from Quebec to New Orleans, but they slighted permanent settlements. French Catholic influence was drastically diluted when France lost the entire area by the treaty of 1763 at the close of the French and Indian War. England received Canada and everything east of the Mississippi, and Spain got Lousiana.

Culturally and religiously, Catholicism left its marks on these regions in varying degrees, but Catholicism did not figure prominently in shaping the national religious ethos. The great Catholic influence came in the late nineteenth century through the immigration of thousands of Southern Europeans, and then it was looked upon as "alien," so much so that Alfred E. Smith's Catholicism was a major factor in his defeat for the presidency in 1928. Until the election of John F. Kennedy as president, being a Catholic was a political liability.

EARLY SENSE OF DIVINE DESTINY

The religious groups along the Atlantic coast largely shaped early colonial religious attitudes, resulting in this country's early Calvinistic orientation. Whatever else might be said about the Calvinists, they had a strong sense of destiny. God was active in human affairs, in history; His providence extended over all; some people, despite their sinfulness, were elected by God to be His agents in the world, to be the means whereby God would glorify Himself on earth. This view is abundantly manifest in the Westminster Confession and in Calvin's numerous commentaries. Calvinists were also strongly convinced that Roman Catholicism had corrupted Christianity and was more a bearer of Satan's ways than of Christ's. This theme is prominent in Calvin's works and in John Foxe's renowned *Book of Martyrs* which appeared in 1563, one of the most influential books in the English language. Foxe openly denounced Roman Catholics for having "slaughtered" and "murdered" thousands of people who resisted the dictates of the Pope. The *Book of Martyrs*, many editions of which were lavishly illustrated, covered Christianity from its early days to the time of Foxe and sensationally aroused passions and prejudices against the Catholics. The Calvinists were also strongly oriented toward the Bible, and easily transferred such biblical notions as "chosen" and "elected" to themselves and their place in God's plan for mankind. Chosenness, anti-Catholicism, and biblical authority passed into the religious ethos of this nation's foundations.

The New World represented a new beginning in which men would have another chance to establish the kingdom of God on earth. This ethos manifested itself in numerous sermons and documents of government. Writing his *History of Plymouth Plantation,* 1620-27, William Bradford noted of the early Pilgrims: "A great hope and inward zeal they had of laying some good foundation, or at least to make some way thereunto, for the propagating and advancing the gospel of the kingdom of Christ in those remote parts of the world." Bradford portrayed the Pilgrims as saints sent by God to battle Satan and establish a colony based on biblical precepts. In the Mayflower Compact of 1620 the Pilgrims swore to establish a colony that would be ruled according to God's ordinances. In 1629 the settlers at Salem accepted a similar agreement: "We covenant with the Lord and with one another; and do bind ourselves in the presence of God to walk together in all his ways, according as he is pleased to reveal himself unto us in his Blessed Word of Truth." The Charlestown-Boston Puritans in 1630 entered into a similar covenant: "Being by God's most wise and good providence brought together into this part of America in the Bay of Massachusetts, . . . we do bind ourselves to walk in all our ways according to the Rule of the Gospel . . . and in mutual love and respect for each other, so near as God shall give us grace."

The Puritans of New England used Deuteronomy 28, and used its promises as justifications of events that unfolded. God's kingdom and their economic-social-religious desires became identified. During the Pequot War of 1637, for example, after killing between 5-700 Indians, Commander Mason remarked, "Thus did the Lord judge among the Heathen, filling the place with dead bodies," and John Underhill added, "We had sufficient light from the Word of God for our proceedings."

The Anglicans of the South differed from the Puritans re royal control of the church, but did not differ re divine providence. Leaders of the Virginia Company believed that the church's ministrations were needed to propagate the Gospel in the New World. Those who settled Jamestown in 1607 were proud Englishmen who wanted to check French expansion and the advance of popery, and to evangelize the Indians. The sealed instructions to the colonists noted: "Lastly and chiefly, the way to prosper and achieve good success is to make yourselves all of one mind for the good of your country and your own, and to serve and fear God, the Giver of all goodness, for every plantation which our Heavenly Father hath not planted shall be rooted out." When De La Warr became the governor of the colony in 1610, his first act was to lead all the colonists in a religious service, and Thomas Dale's *Lawes Divine, Morall and Maritall* established "divine" law for civic affairs, and "martial" law for the church.[1] Army officers were to see "that the Almightie God bee duly and daily served" and that prayer services be attended. Perry Miller noted in his *Errand into the Wilderness* that the settlers in the South had virtually the same frame of reference as the Puritans. Alexander Whitaker, one of Virginia's earliest divines, was an outspoken predestinarian.[2] Virginia's charter required government by the "ecceliastical laws of England" and that policy was offically maintained throughout the colonial period. The popularly elected assembly legally established Anglicanism and bound the colonists to conformity with the Church of England. Virginia became a crown colony in 1624. After 1636 citizens had to pay tithes, and only Anglicans could vote. But something else had also been introduced into the South — slavery. The indentured blacks who arrived in 1619 were the beginning of a slave system that gradually changed the South. Not that the Southerners did not feel themselves directed and chosen by God, but that "the church became inescapably associated with social privilege," and it was this prevailing pattern of privilege that caused the church to decline in popular influence.[3] Agricultural needs prompted a system of cheap, involuntary labor. While many Anglicans objected to theological justification of this change, it too could be justified on the basis of Deuteronomy 28. The South became increasingly prosperous; they were being blessed for keeping the commandments of God. The dream of America as a chosen people did not disappear, but the Anglican control gradually decreased. Privilege was for the few, and other people might well interpret the Bible differently. During the Civil War, people on both sides were convinced that God would decide the victor. Baptists, even more Calvinistic than the Anglicans, eventually became the most numerous Protestant group in the South, further strengthening the divine mission ethos.

Neither the Anglicans, Pilgrims, nor Puritans favored religious toleration. They made landholding and church membership in good standing requirements for voting. This caused serious tension later because even those who were not church members had to pay tithes. Dissenters were generally scorned. Wrote Nathaniel Ward, "All Familists, Antinomians, Anabaptists, and other Enthusiasts, shall have free Liberty to keep away from us, and such as will come to be gone as fast as they can, the sooner the better." The "godly" settlements of the Anglicans, Pilgrims and Puritans were far from free and open. Non-orthodox, contentious outsiders were not welcome, especially if they were Catholics or Quakers.

Massachusetts Puritanism spawned other colonies, including New Hampshire and Maine. Thomas Hooker and John Davenport led settlers into Connecticut, and Roger Williams and Anne Hutchinson led groups into

Rhode Island. The Bible was basic to the government of each, but Roger Williams was the first to advocate religious toleration; he belived the church should be voluntary in membership and that the government should confine itself to civil matters. In his *Bloudy Tenent of Persecution,* 1644, he vigorously upheld right of conscience, even for Roman Catholics. He did not advocate a national, coercive church, but he did not believe that God was any the less active in what he was doing. Anne Hutchinson shared many of his views, and these dissenting Baptist convictions about religion were exported to other settlements.

George Calvert (Lord Baltimore) tried but failed to establish religious toleration in his colony along the Potomac River, Maryland, even though in 1649 he persuaded the Assembly to pass an act of religious toleration for Christians. When Maryland became a crown colony in 1691, toleration for non-Trinitarians and Roman Catholics was a thing of the past. Catholics lost their right to vote, and could not legally say mass or baptize non-Catholic children.

William Penn, a convert to Quakerism in 1667, sought to establish a colony that would support political and religious freedom. He had notable success, treated the Indians as equals, and attracted many settlers. But his policies allowed slavery which became a rending issue in the 1700s. Delaware which became independent in 1702 was part of Penn's "holy experiment."

Lord John Berkeley and Sir George Carteret published agreements for complete freedom of conscience and rule by popular assembly to attract settlers to New Jersey, but by 1702 the whole of New Jersey had for a variety of reasons become a royal colony. A similar story transpired in the Carolinas where dissidents from Virginia sought relief from Anglicanism, and staved off establishment of Anglicanism for some forty years. In 1729 the proprietors sold the Carolinas back to the crown, which divided them into North and South.

When James Oglethorpe founded Savannah in 1733 Roman Catholics were not accorded religious freedom, although it was given to all others. Anglicanism was favored but was not established until 1755, three years after Georgia became a royal colony.

From colony to colony the pattern varied, but the notion remained that God had opened up a wilderness in which his ancient biblical promises were at last to be realized. This notion pervaded those colonies that allowed relative toleration and those that did not. Despite differences, the mystique prevailed that God was using the New World to achieve his mysterious purposes in history. Success in pushing back the frontiers increased the convictions, and those very same wilderness frontier conditions sponsored a sense of self-reliance and democratic equality of all men under God. Roman Catholicism was hardly a viable part of the panorama. Roman Catholicism was generally regarded as the problem which the New World was seeking to avoid. A major lesson learned from this early experience in America was that while all believed strongly in the providence and guidance of God, no single religious polity was strong enough to unite all the settlements. Experience gradually taught the colonists that toleration was a necessity, for they needed the aid of one another in surmounting the difficulties facing them in America. The Enlightenment of the Age of Reason added to the conviction that religion was needed to help people relate morally but that the specifics of dogmas only added to the contentions of mankind. Rationalistic latitudinarianism coincided increasingly with religious experience to open up a new relationship between the church and state in America.

PLURALISM AND FREEDOM UNDER CIVIL LAW

The growing difficulties between England and the colonists in America eroded some of the older convictions about religious exclusiveness and taught the colonists that economic and political survival might well depend on finding a basis on which religious cooperation could take place. That basis found expression in the Declaration of Independence: "We hold these truths to be self-evident, that all men are created equal, that they are endowed by their Creator with certain unalienable rights, that among these are life, liberty, and the pursuit of happiness. That to secure these rights, governments are instituted among men, deriving their just powers from the consent of the governed. That whenever any form of government becomes destructive of these ends, it is the right of the people to alter or to abolish it, and to institute new government, laying its foundation on such principles and organizing its powers in such form, as to them shall seem most likely to effect their safety and happiness." In the Declaration a general appeal was made to "the Laws of Nature and Nature's God," "the Supreme Judge of the World," and "Divine Providence," but specific forms of religion and references to the Bible were not included.

Just as the frontier realities and the economic struggle with England brought the colonies together on one level, so religious experience tended to bring them together on another. Rationalism and Deism had strong advocates in Benjamin Franklin, Tom Paine, Jonathan Mayhew, James Madison, and Thomas Jeferson, all of whom disliked establishment religion, and all of whom figured prominently in the drive toward independence. Their contentions combined with a variety of Protestant arguments for toleration, a general distrust of ecclesiastical control, and frontier individualism to produce a feeling that no one should be compelled in matters of conscience, that the state should have a core of morality but that religious practices should be voluntary. The Great Awakening which cut across denominational lines from New England to Georgia tended to show that God's activity in the world could not be confined to formulated beliefs, and that personal emotional conversion was more signifcant than denominational membership. In their zeal to win converts, the revivalists largely ignored denominational differences. Their success seemed to verify the presence of God's spirit. George Whitefield was a staunch Anglican, but he virtually shunned his church's polity; if one confessed love for Jesus Christs, that was enough. That less than ten percent of the people were church-affiliated seems to indicate that many people could accept a core of morality that had parallels in both Nature and the Bible, but could not accept a specific exclusive form of Christianity. Benjamin Franklin praised the revivalists for their exhortations to good citizenship. but did not praise their preaching for conversion to a particular church.

Mutual dangers and expectations slowly drew the colonists together. By the time of the framing of the Constitution, no church was powerful enough to demand national establishment, but a reasonable, Christian morality as a basis for government seemed to prevail. Rationalism on both sides of the Atlantic had grown strong in the eighteenth century. Revelation and Reason coalesced on a kind of practical morality, and loyalty to one nation, under God, took precedence over any single religious form. Logically and experientially, this meant no established churches, and this stance was embodied in the First Amendment to the Constitution in 1791: "Congress shall make no law respecting an establishment of religion, or prohibiting the free exercise thereof; or abridging the freedom of speech or of the press; or the right of the people peaceably to assemble, and to petition the government for a redress of grievances." Since all seemed to be working harmoniously toward the same end, the remaining establishments quietly disappeared, Connecticut in 1818, New Hampshire, 1819, and Massachusetts, 1833.

The Declaration of Independence and the First Amendment set the parameters for church-state relations in the United States. These documents bequeathed a legacy of religious toleration and pluralism under civil authority. Neither the toleration nor the pluralism resulted so much from piety as from practicality; many groups continued to claim that they alone possessed sole truth. However, they relinquished outward coercion. By different routes they had come to a consensus to propagate their views only by persuasion; no one should be coerced in religious convictions. This left the state as the guarantor of religious toleration, constitutionally unable to aid or hinder any religious expressions. A general ethos developed that God had called forth a new nation to be the bearer of His righteousness; the whole nation would embody Christian convictions.

7

However, the ethos was decidedly Protestant, not Jewish, not Roman Catholic. An undergirding of morality was commonly assumed to be necessary for government. Deists, rationalists, and traditionalists might quarrel over the nature of God and worship, but they could agree in general on morality as a base for government. The Bible through revelation and Nature through reason seemed to disclose similar laws. Although Tom Paine and Elihu Parker might object, people could generally agree to the teachings and morals of Jesus. Sound government demanded as much, and it was on this level that the Protestant churches and the non-affiliated coalesced. No single church, but rather the nation was hailed as the umbrella of God's chosen people on their manifest destiny. Strong rivalries existed and the line between church and state often became blurred, but under civil law all could unite.

This ethos proved to be extremely beneficial to most groups. But not to all. Roman Catholics were eyed suspiciously for well over a century and a half. The national ethos was predominantly Protestant. The public school system promoted this ethos, not in a sectarian sense but as part of the moral fiber of the nation, as a foundation for all. Horace Mann wanted the Gospel included in all courses of study in his schools, not for its religious statement of good news but as a base for peace and unity. Protestants accepted the public school system because they identified their own aims with those of the nation. The Presbyterians abandoned their 250 parochial schools early in the nineteenth century because they viewed the public schools as fostering almost identical goals as their own. Publications such as E. S. Ely's *The Duty of Freemen to Elect Christian Rulers* appeared. Pulpits rang with chauvinistic chosenness. Says Sydney Mead in *The Lively Experiment*, "Under the system of official separation of church and state the denominations eventually found themselves as completely identified with nationalism and their country's political and economic systems as had ever been known in Christendom."[4] Even during the Civil War, the feeling existed on both sides that God would decide the outcome. After the conflict, both North and South continued to promote an underlying sense of divine Protestant destiny.

This meshing of nationalism and Protestantism accounted in large measure for the anti-Catholic feeling that manifested itself before and after the Civil War, in the South as well as the North. Bishop John Hughes (d. 1864) opposed public schools and sought public funds for Roman Catholic parochial schools because he perceived this meshing regardless of the separation clause in the First Amendment. Protestant reaction to this Catholic drive prompted further development of the public school system and bans on aid to sectarian schools, and the rapid increase in Catholic immigration engendered widespread fears of internal subversion. By 1860 the Catholic population in this country numbered well over 3,000,000 and the Roman Catholic Church was the largest single church body in the United States. This fact heightened Protestant nativism to the point of alarm. It showed itself in the preaching and writings of Lyman Beecher, Horace Bushnell, Samuel F. B. Morse, and many others. Catholic missions were branded as subversive infiltrations to overthrow American democracy, the Roman Catholic Church itself was regarded as an extension of a foreign government, and Catholics were charged with undermining America's democratic processes. Mob action errupted in Boston and other cities. Groups such as the Native American Party, The Order of the Star-Spangled Banner, and the Know-Nothings sought to keep Catholics out of public office. In 1856 these groups ran Millard Fillmore as President. After the Civil War, anti-Roman Catholicism again flared throughout the nation. Historic papal claims to control of temporal as well as spiritual matters made Protestants suspect virtually everything Catholic. The Ku Klux Klan, formed to keep blacks "in their place," was violently anti-Catholic until well into the twentieth century and was strong in the North as well as the South. The American Protective Association, organized in Iowa in 1887, sought to curb Roman Catholic political power, limit Catholic immigration, and deny public funds to parochial schools. When Pope Leo XIII rebuffed Cardinal Gibbons and other Catholic leaders in 1899 for trying to "Americanize" Catholicism in the United States, nativists felt that their fears had been vindicated. The bloody strikes that racked this nation in the 1880s and 90s had anti-Catholic overtones inasmuch as Catholic immigrants comprised much of the labor force. Mormons and others who did not readily fit into the national concensus also suffered violent attacks.

The national Protestant mission seemed stronger than ever by the end of the nineteenth century. John D. Rockefeller, G. F. Baer, Andrew Carnegie, and other entrepreneurs of business regarded their wealth as God's providential blessing, and the poverty of others as God's judgment in keeping with Deutronomy 28. Henry Ward Beecher, Horace Bushnell, Josiah Strong, and Russell Conwell explained poverty as a consequence of vice. Indiana's Senator Albert J. Beveridge extolled America as a redeemer nation when at the turn into the twentieth century he spoke to his fellow senators: "God has not been preparing the English-speaking and Teutonic peoples for a thousand years for nothing but vain and idle self-contemplation and self-admiration. No. He has made us master organizers of the world to establish system where chaos reigned. He has given us the spirit of progress to overwhelm the forces of reaction throughout the earth. He has made us adept in government that we may administer government among the savage and senile peoples. Were it not for such a force as this the world would relapse into barbarism and night. And of all our race He has marked out the American people as His chosen nation to finally lead in the redemption of the world."[5]

9

Religious pluralism under the state has kept America free for the most part of the religious strife that so often marred the countries of Europe. Some 300 religious groups have established their right to privileges under the Constitution. Supreme Court decisions have thrown light on the frequently blurred line between church and state. Can taxes be used to finance parochial schools? Can prayers be said in classrooms? Can nuns teach in their official garbs in public schools? Can children be released from public schools for religious instruction in their respective churches? Can church property be taxed? These questions vexed the churches, but by and large they reflected conflicts among the churches vying for advantages with the national government.

The larger question of national sovereignty as a religion was virtually ignored. This nation's religious chauvinism was what Syndey Mead and others called the "Religion of the Republic," a common core of morality on which the various church groups could agree for the sake of national order and security. It eroded belief in the ultimate signifcance of any denominational doctrine or polity, and fostered an attitude that the state alone was really significant. Patriotism superceded religion, even though a concensus core of morality was deemed necessary to the functioning of government. In 1952 Dwight David Eisenhower said, "Our government makes no sense unless it is founded in a deeply felt religious faith, and I don't care what it is."[6] This has been sloganized on bumper stickers as "Love it or leave it," and "My country, right or wrong." Robert Bellah and other historians have characterized this as religion of the state, with its own rituals, hymns, and saints.[7] This situation poses questions about the ultimate viability of religious pluralism under the state.

Two world wars and then Vietnam prompted doubt about this nation as the bearer of divine righteousness. World War I did not make the world safe for demoncracy, World War II spawned as many problems as it alleviated, and Vietnam left us ignominiously thwarted by a nation relatively unknown. Success after success in the past had verified the national ethos, as if God were watching over His own. But tragic failure in Vietnam laid bare an emptiness that many had come to suspect. When Watergate unfolded with all its implications, with its threat to the very essence of democratic processes, disillusionment spread — disillusionment about goals, ideals, morality, trust, chosenness, and identity. The political fabric was suddenly revealed as tawdry; millions felt betrayed. When President Gerald Ford pardoned Richard M. Nixon and took no action for those working under Nixon, he displayed not so much forgiveness of God as an intuition to protect the state.

The freedom of religious pluralism under civil authority has served this nation well, but national sovereignty has tended to displace religious commitments. Whether a viable church-state relationship can be maintained has been jeopardized. That no single church should have sovereign authority has been at the very heart of the American experiment. But that state sovereignty harbors as many problems as church sovereignty is only now becoming apparent. A state that holds itself above moral laws easily becomes a tyranny, with the loss of freedom, as dictatorships have repeatedly demonstrated. What rights does the state inherently have? Does it have the right to sovereignty, no matter what the conflict with religious conviction? The question surfaced in World War II and also in Vietnam. Nazi war criminals repeatedly justified their actions with "We were following orders." The Nuremberg trials declared that "following orders" was not justification enough for the killing of millions of Jews simply because they were Jews. The Nuremberg trials pointed to a higher law. Lieutenant William Calley pleaded "orders" for the wanton killings he was accused of in Vietnam. If following "orders" is not strictly maintained, if each person is morally bound to judge the commands he is given by superior officers, then an army can hardly be viable. One might well be religiously obligated not even to join, or to register for the draft, on the ground that such action would lead to moral compromise. This happened during the Vietnam struggle. Thousands went underground, thousands fled to Canada and Sweden, thousands went to jail. Conscientious objection was extremely hard to establish with draft boards. Whenever the fate of the nation is at stake, religion takes second place. Amnesty has not been granted those who protested the war, even though subsequent disclosures have revealed that America's entry into the war was based on manipulation and lies.

It is too early to say whether naked state sovereignty will prevail in the future, but that we have come to the edge of this possibility is abundantly clear. Religious freedom cannot be allowed to infringe on the freedom of others, and it cannot be allowed to subvert the final authority of the state. On the other hand, state sovereignty cannot be allowed to be idolatrous. Therein is the church-state tension as I see it for the future. Ancient Rome was tolerant of many religions; however, it demanded worship of the emperor as divine, emperor worship being symbolic of imperial unity. The early Christians could not do that. Hitler led Germany into a similar situation; a few resisted; millions of Jews died. Whether such an impasse will develop in the United States remains to be seen.

The widespread erosion of truth and reality in our century has complicated this predicament. Subjectivity and relativity have become so obvious in our assertions of truth and reality that uncertainty is a mark of our times. This epistemological erosion has affected science, philosophy, religion, and everyday mores. What is right and what is wrong? What is true and untrue? By what standard? If literature, art, philosophy, and religion, suicide rates and crime statistics are indicators of our cultural ethos, then a kind of meaninglessness and uncertainty pervades our culture, leaving cynicism, indifference, and violence in its wake. In 1961 Gabriel Vahanian published *The Death of God: The Culture of Our Post-Christian Era*. Protestants such as T. J. J. Altizer and William Hamilton in the middle sixties popularized the "Death" of God, engendering doubt about almost all beliefs in the minds of Protestants. The authority of the Pope has been severely questioned in Roman Catholicism, and many traditions have fallen. In 1966, reacting to the horrors of Auschwitz, Rabbi Richard Rubenstein argued that God is a "Nothingness" and that man's destiny is simply death.

Church-state relations have been complicated by this kind of milieu. Sovereignty of any kind has become suspect. Blacks, various minorities, interest groups, and others have questioned chauvinism and its basis. Yet society has to have order to exist. When that order is not obtainable on a concensus basis, then conformity by force becomes necessary. How religious convictions will fare in such a situation raises unresolved problems for church and state.

In the first two hundred years of colonization, an ethos of divine mission pervaded our culture. In the first hundred years of our bicentennial, that divine mission operated under constitutionally guaranteed freedom of religion, even though Catholics and others experienced difficulty. In the second hundred years of our bicentennial, the meaning of separation of church and state has come under sharp scrutiny. To what extent can churches legitimately acknowledge state soveriegnty? What are its limits? The American experiment has not yet given answers to the questions.[8]

NOTES:

1.   Ahlstrom, Sydney E., *A Religious History of the American People* (New Haven: Yale University Press, 1972) pp. 184 ff.

2.   *Ibid.*, pp. 186 ff.

3.   *Ibid.*, p. 196.

4.   Mead, Sydney, *The Lively Experiment* (New York: Harper & Row, Publishers, 1963), p. 157.

5.   See Ernest L. Tuveson, *Redeemer Nation* (Chicago: University of Chicago Press, 1968), p. vii.

6.   See Sydney Mead, *The Nation with the Soul of a Church* (New York: Harper and Row, Publishers, 1975), p. 25.

7.   See *Religion in America*, edited by William G. McLoughlin and Robert N. Bellah (Boston: Houghton Mifflin, 1968).

8.   For other works touching church-state relations see R. A. Billington, *The Protestant Crusade, 1800-1860: Origins of American Nativism*; Robert T. Handy *A Christian America*; Withrop S. Hudson, *Religion in America*; Martin E. Marty, *Righteous Empire: Protestant Experience in America*; Frederick Sontag and J. K. Roth, *The American Religious Experience*; and Anson P. Stokes, *Church and State in the United States.*

THE BLACK RELIGIOUS EXPERIENCE IN AMERICA: A UNION OF TWO WORLDS

By CHARLES SHELBY ROOKS

The celebration of the American Bicentennial this year has caused a widespread debate to develop in the black communitiy over whether blacks should participate in the prolonged ritual of celebration of the American life and dream. Attitudes of black Americans range from the assertion, on the one hand, that blacks should completely ignore the year-long celebration to the idea, on the other hand, that each event should be the occasion for dramatic black protest against America's continued inhumane treatment of the descendants of African tribes. Lerone Bennett, resident historian for *Ebony* magazine, is one who believes blacks should not participate, while J. H. Jackson, President of the National Baptist Convention, Inc., the largest black denomination of the United States, believes they should, and echoes the words of James Weldon Johnson at the celebration of the fiftieth anniversary of the Emancipation Proclamation:

> This land is ours by right of birth,
> This land is ours by right of toil,
> We helped to turn its virgin earth,
> Our sweat is in its fruitful soil.

Since blacks have contributed so much to the building of this nation, so this argument runs, they have as much right as anyone to celebrate its bicentennial.

The debate of this issue is evidence of the ever-present agony in black America over what the nature of black existence in this land should be. Blacks began their existence here under the awful brutality of slavery, and have been denied full access to "life, liberty and the pursuit of happiness" even to the present day. The question which has perpetually haunted black America is: What does life mean in the midst of unchanging inhumanity and oppression? During much of the history of black America, this question was answered in fundamentally religious ways which undergirded social, political and economic responses. That was so because the African who came to these shores was a religious being who viewed life holistically and could not separate his life into secular and spiritual spheres. The pragmatic responses to the question have included five ideas: (1) integration or assimilation, (2) revolution or rebellion, (3) separatism and ultimately black nationalism on these shores, (4) coexistence, and (5) a return to Africa. Each response has had its proponents, most of whom arose from positions of religious leadership within the black community. All of these ideas continue to be found in black America as the agonizing question of the meaning of black existence here remains unresolved.

In the present debate over black participation in the bicentennial celebration, the issue is, in part, the historic overt violence of whites against blacks. Visible physical violence is plain to all who read history. The slave system in America was never a benign, benevolent social structure, and no amount of rhetoric can ever make it so. Slaveowners held the absolute right of life and death over their property — which was what slaves were — and could exercise that power without any sort of legal review. Thousands of Africans died on slave ships en route to America. Thousands more died on slave plantations here. After the Civil War, the power of life and death continued to be held in the hands of white America. In the South, lynchings were a fact of black life constantly up to the 1940s as bands of self-appointed whites decided among themselves who among the black community required the purge of death. Even during the 1960 s, lynchings continued to mark the civil rights struggle, broadened this time to include whites who were foolish enough to aid the black cause. The North was more sophisticated in its use of the power of life and death. In this century the race riot in many large cities with significant black populations was the chief tactic for control. While that may sound strange, since most riots were begun by blacks themselves, riots such as the one in Harlem in the 1920s resulted in the deaths of large numbers of blacks at the hands of police brutality run wild. It is significant that black violence in American history nearly always was violence against **property**, but white violence against blacks nearly always was violence against **persons.** In view of the physical violence so constantly a part of black existence in this nation, what are the clues to the meaning of that existence? Why should blacks **celebrate** their history in such a country? These are the questions at issue.

Equally important as the problem of physical violence has been the accompanying spiritual violence which represented the attempt to alter the whole psyche of the black community. Slavery in America was a structural experiment with radical surgery upon the mind of the African newcomers. The initial assault upon the mind was the terrible condition of the slave ship — humans beings packed by hundreds and bound by chains in the hold of a ship, unable to move, unable to bathe, forced to release body waste on themselves and their neighbor, without air or light, and with little food. The second assault was the slave market where they were stripped naked, were bought and sold, and separated from their friends and kinsmen. The third assault was the plantation and the need to reorient themselves completely to a new existence, to learn a new language and customs, to develop new relationships both white and black, and where the prospect of the whip was a constant companion.

These assaults upon the mind were partially physical, of course, but the physical produced drastic psychological effects as well. The slaveowner was not content with those initial acts, however. In order to insure the docility of the African, a series of non-physical violences to personhood ensued. The opportunity to practice tribal religion was completely forbidden. African customs were not allowed, and only English could be spoken. Slaves were not permitted to learn or hear anything of their former continent. And so forth. Finally, it was declared that blacks were not human beings at all, but the creation by God himself of a subspecies of human life, lacking the intelligence and abilities of whites, fit only to be hewers of wood and drawers of water. The attempt to dehumanize blacks completely and obliterate their history represents the only occasion in history in which slavery reached such base form. Over the long history of this globe, no other instance of slavery had as its goal such brutal and systematic dehumanization.

In view of this history, some of it quite recent, it is not surprising that blacks themselves continue to agonize over the meaning of their existence in this nation, or that their responses to the question are so varied. At the research and scholarship level, one attempt to respond to the question has been recognition of the need to recover the truth of obscured or distorted black history. Back in 1882, George Washington Williams, then a young black man of thirty-three, wrote a book entitled, *History of the Negro Race in America, 1619-1880.* In his preface, he explained that he wrote the history for five reasons: (1) because blacks had been the most vexatious problem in North America from the time of its discovery down to the (then) present day; (2) because he wanted to reveal how the colored pople had always displayed a matchless patriotism and an incomparable heroism in the cause of Americans whenever the nation was attacked; (3) in order to give Americans more correct ideas of the colored people; (4) to incite the black population itself to greater effort in the struggle for citizenship and manhood; and (5) because he was not a blind panegyrist of his race nor a partisan apologist, but from a love for the truth of history. Williams articulated what have continued to be the motivations of black recoverers of history up to the present day. It is a recognition of the need for the black scholar or researcher always to take cognizance of the social, psychological, and political aspects of his endeavors. The discovery of truth is not enough by itself, for even undiluted truth, if such exists, has far-reaching implications.

The most difficult problem facing the researcher is whether there are sufficient extant materials upon which to base a judgment. Obviously the conditions of slavery were not conducive to the formulation and preservation of written record among blacks themselves, and whites had particular reasons not to do so. After slavery there were not large numbers of persons who could write since formal education had previously been grossly neglected by slave-owners, and the development of an educated class takes considerable time. The problem can be put best by suggesting a single set of questions: In the midst of the awful assault upon the psyche that slavery represented, what happened to African understandings and consciousness of the meaning of life that slaves brought with them? Did these ideas disappear entirely? Were even portions of them retained? What actually occurred? Not only so, what happened with the succeeding generations of blacks who were born on these shores but who had no personal memory of Africa? Slavery on these shores is more than three hundred fifty years old. Do any vestiges of Africanism remain in the present life of the black community? Are there primary sources to which the researcher can turn for data?

The debate about the continuing existence of African survivals in America was begun by W. E. B. DuBois at the turn of the present century and continued to the last decade. Today there is little conjecture over whether African survivals exist. The issue is the discovery of their extent. More and more primary sources are bing uncovered and put into print today than ever before. DuBois' 1903 book, *The Negro Church,* for instance, noted the way in which Christianity, as presented and taught to blacks by American whites, was designed to make them passive, but stated his belief that the nature of black religion was actually quite different than whites believed. This differnece was due not only to what Du Bois believed to be the political character of black religion, but also to the survival of the remnants of African tribal life. He concluded that the first gatherings of the slaves for religious purposes, away from white supervision, were something other than Christian worship. They were in fact adaptations of African religious gatherings, the vestiges of which remained after these gatherings bore the name Christian. Four decades later, Melville Herskovits demonstrated in more detail that African survivals can be demonstrated in religion and in every other instance of black life in the United States in his book, *The Myth of the Negro Past.* Since that time only the late black sociologist E. Franklin Frazier has articulated an opposite view. It was Frazier's contention that all African cultural forms had disappeared. He wrote in 1939:

> Probably never before in history has a people been so nearly stripped of its social heritage as the Negroes who were brought to America . .

16

Of the habits and customs as well as the hopes and fears that
characterized the life of their forebears in Africa, nothing remains.[1]

But if Frazier were still alive today, he would have difficulty maintaining that position because an increasingly large amount of primary data
has been uncovered by recent researchers which supports the DuBois-
Herskovits stance.

With all that as necessary background, the thesis which stands at the
center of this article is two-fold: (1) that religion was absolutely crucial to
African life and has also been crucial to Afro-American life; and (2) that
the religions of the Afro-American is a synthesis of African tribal religion
and American Christianity which is unique in the world. Recent research
and scholarship would support both these ideas.

One of the problems connected with the development of this thesis is
that up to the present most interpreters of black religious experience have
been whites who have not understood what they viewed. In Africa, as well
as in other parts of the world, native religion has nearly always been written about by white Christian missionaries who were not intellectually
equipped to understand religious phenomenology and who allowed their
Christian and Western biases to color completely their observations. The
language they used about such religious phenomena is itself an indication
of bias. African tribal religion was described as "heathen," a prejorative
and negative term. Even scientific language used such words as "animism"
to describe the phenomena, again a word with pejorative overtones. Little
or no attempt was ever made to value the religious customs and experiences of Africans positively. Christian evanglism required the destruction of primary belief structures in any given culture and then attempted
to impose Christian and Western belief structures which often were completely at variance with the needs of those cultures.

The death of colonialism in Africa has meant the possibility for radical
reinterpretation of the value of African tribal religions. On the African
continent today an increasing number of Africans are taking a fresh look
at those phenomena. One of these is John Mbiti, who has made a study of
some 300 peoples from all over Africa outside the traditionally Christian
and Muslim communities. In his book, *African Religions and Philosophy*,
Mbiti makes two principal contentions about African religions. One is that
religion is a total experience which engulfs an individual's entire being. He
claims that the African lived in a religious innocence which meant that all
of his activites were imbued with religious meaning and significance.
Religion was, therefore, the "whole system of being" for each African. The
Western separation of the religious and the secular is nowhere to be observed in African religion. Mbiti's second contention is even more startling
to Western scholars: that in "all these societies, without a single exception,
people have a notion of God as the Supreme Being," and "this is the most

17

minimal and fundamental idea about, God, found in all African societies."[2] Obviously, the point of contention here is the observation by Westerners of a variety of other spiritual beings and divinities in African tribal religions, the identification of physical places with worship, and the deification of some tribal or national heroes. It is Mbiti's belief and observation, however, that in each case such beings are understood by the African to be created by the one Supreme God, and they cannot be perceived apart from that creation. As comprehended by the new African scholars, then, African tribal religions were central to the very daily existence of the people, and focused on the one Supreme God and the varieties of ways in which that God manifested himself in life.

Two black American authors in this decade have spotlighted the effect of this religious centrality to daily life for the slave who came to America. Cecil W. Cone in *The Identity Crisis in Black Theology* and Gayraud S. Wilmore in *Black Religion and Black Radicalism* have attempted to show how the background of African religion and the encounter with Christianity on these shores produced a new and unique religious experience that is continuous to the present. It is inconceibable to both that persons who understood life primarily in religious terms would suddenly give up the centrality of religious meaning and values even under the oppression of slavery. While slaves could not practice their old religions, even the bearability of the new religion was conditioned by their memory of the old one. Thus, the idea of a Creator God, as known through the Judeo-Christian tradition, held enough similarity to the Supreme God they had already known for the new God of the Christian religion to have credibility and acceptability. What was required was a re-creation and new understanding of the customs and traditions of the new religion. Cone calls this the "encounter with the Almighty Sovereign God" on these shores. As that encounter with God occurred, some of the African ways were adapted to the new religious condition. Such ritual customs as the praise house, the ring dance, the special tree and praying ground, the field prayers, etc., all are adjustments of tribal religious customs to the practice of Christianity by blacks in the slave period. What is important, however, is not the adjustments themselves but the continued importance of religion in the daily lives of the people. It was this fact which enabled the slaves to find meaning for their existence in the midst of brutality and dehumanization. Just as it was the means by which life itself was preserved and maintained in the old country, so religion in the new world provided a method for understanding the terrible conditions of the new existence and contributed to the survival of the people, for only as life has consistent meaning and value can religious persons survive the problems and difficulties of life.

It is important to remember that the encounter with God of the

Christian religion and the adaptation of religious practices to the new faith was a continuing necessity up to the middle of the nineteenth century. The slave trade continued almost up to the Civil War. Indeed, the period from 1800 to 1850 was the period of the heaviest traffic in slavery. The large numbers of Africans who came to America in this period were forced to reorient their lives. Thus, the description of what occurred was alive in the memories of those who underwent that experience, and this represented a large number of persons who survived into the twentieth century. Their memory also influenced those who were born on this continent and who had no direct recollection of Africa. Thus, the value of religion as the central means for the preservation of life continued the transforming process in the black community.

Few observers of the religious experience of black Americans up to this time have paid sufficient attention to the similarities and differences between the institutional forms of black religion, usually but not entirely Christian, and what could be called black folk or even civil religion. In both instances what developed was different from the religious experiences of whites, therefore in some sense unique, and both continued to have elements of African customs and practices interwoven with the cultic practices of America. Gayraud Wilmore argues, for example, that the **defining** characteristic of spirituality in African religions was the freedom of the person, and that the essential ingredient of black religion in America was always the desire for freedom. He maintains that by the beginning of this century other religious viewpoints and practices were taking shape in the black community which turned the mainstream of the black quest for freedom in three different directions: (1) a Christian stream, institutionalized primarily in the independent black churches; (2) a stream which threw off religious influences altogether, but which still owed many of its concepts to essentially religious ideas; and (3) a stream, characterized by W. E. B. DuBois and the NAACP, that was not explicitly religious but which made use of the Christian churches in moving toward the middle-class goal of removing all barriers toward full participation in American society. Since the issue of freedom is so central to Afro-American understanding of life, the development of these differing streams in the quest for freedom resulted in what Wilmore calls the "dechristianization of black religion." However the three streams diverged, and Wilmore is constrained to ask whether in the future black religion in America will remain essentially Christian. Whether it does or not, he says,

> The radical faiths of Malcolm (X) and Martin (Luther King, Jr.) coalesce in the opaque depths of a Black spirituality that is neither Protestant nor Catholic, Christian nor Islamic in its essence, but comprehends and transcends these ways of believing in God by experiencing his real presence, by becoming one with him in suffering, in struggle and in the celebration of the liberation of man.[3]

Wilmore claims that this religious "common sense, sagacity and style of life of the folk" goes far beyond the formal and informal religious occasions and events either in the fields or in the churchs, and continues to permeate the entire spectrum of life and activity in the black community. As much as the formal practice of Christian religion, this substratum of religion has influenced the long struggle of blacks to be free on this continent. Rooted in African consciousness, it further developed on this continent and has its special uniqueness among the blacks of the African Diaspora in the new world.

The central assertion of contemporary black American scholars, however, is that the encounter of African tribal religion and American Protestant Christianity produced a unique religion on these shores. While there may be some continuing discussion of the elements of that uniqueness, nearly every black author on the present scene makes that assumption the basis for his or her work. That fact is in stark contrast to the traditional assumptions of white historians and sociologists of religion, nearly every one of whom interprets black religious experience, particularly its institutionalized form, the church, in the light of what are believed to be similar sectarian experiences among whites. This is a conflicting approach to scholarly interpretation of the data that is not likely to be quickly resolved since both blacks and whites are bound so much to their own cultures.

Perhaps the most articulate argument for the uniqueness of black Christianity is to be found in James H. Cone's new book, *God of the Oppressed.* In it he argues a variety of different theolgies and thought forms which are fundamental among blacks that are not to be found in white Christianity. On the one hand, Cone asserts, the difference between whites and blacks religiously in America is sociological. Blacks worked from sunup to nightfall and had no time for philosophical and theological discourse. The language which they used was not the language of rational discourse but the language of stories. They told their religious truth in concrete and vivid pictures that brought to light God's dealings with them. White theology in America remains skeptical about truth in story form. Black theology, however, has always meant retelling and proclaiming the story of God's mighty acts in history. On the other hand, Cone maintains that the difference is also theological. While whites ponder the existence of God and define Jesus as a spiritual Saviour, the deliverer of people from sin and guilt, the God of black Christianity was involved with the pople in the struggle for **physical** freedom in this world. If God could deliver Israel from Pharaoh's army and Daniel from the lion's den, then surely he could deliver black people from the slavery and oppression of America. These are but two differences which represent radically divergent religious content in what are alleged by white scholars to be similar encounters with

God by blacks and whites on these shores.

Cone goes yet another step by arguing that the divine revelation in the biblical message was directed **exclusively** at the oppressed of the earth and that, because blacks are the most oppressed in American society, God has especially favored them with His presence. He says,

> Jesus was not simply a nice fellow who happened to like the poor. Rather his actions have their origin in God's eternal being. They represent a new vison of divine freedom, climaxed with the cross and the resurrection, wherein God breaks into history for the liberation of slaves from societal oppression. Jesus' actions represent God's will not to let his creation be destroyed by non-creative powers. The cross and the resurrection show that the freedom promised is now available in Jesus Christ.[4]

It was this reality which the black Christian perceived in the midst of oppression. Cone believes that this represents a tremendously radical departure from the religious perceptions of whites and is one essential difference which causes black Christianity to be a unique experience on these shores. He is but one of the new breed of black scholars who wrestle fundamentally with the religious meaning of black existence in America.

Clearly much remains to be done before either the concrete indications of African survivals or the elements of black religious uniqueness are adequately catalogued. It is essential, however, that the task be undertaken for the sake of the black community itself. While there is validity in articulating black religious experience for the world of white scholarship, the more fundamental need is for contemporary blacks, particularly black youth, to understand more clearly their tremendous heritage of religion and the source of strength it provided without which neither the African in the homeland under colonial rule nor the black slave in America could have survived and grown both in numbers and in the unceasing will to freedom everywhere.

NOTES:

1. Frazier, E. Franklin, *The Negro Family in the United States* (Chicago: University of Chicago Press, 1939), p. 15.

2. Mbiti, John S., *African Religions and Philosphy* (New York: Anchor Books, 1970), pp. 37, 39.

3. Wilmore, Gayraud S., *Black Religion and Black Radicalism* (Garden City, N.Y.: Doubleday, 1972), p. 261.

4. Cone, James H., *God of the Oppressed* (New York: Seabury Press, 1975), p. 81.

ANNOTATED BIBLIOGRAPHY

Cone, Cecil W., *The Identity Crisis in Black Theology* (Nashville: AMEC Press, 1975).
> Cone is the older brother of James H. Cone. This is his doctoral dissertation and discusses the sources and foundations of black theology and the difficulties in the works of Joseph H. Washington, James Cone and J. Deotis Roberts, who are earlier writers in the field.

Cone, James H., *God of the Oppressed* (New York: Seabury Press, 1975).
> The most radical of black theologians and the one who has attracted the most attention, this is the fourth book by Cone in the last eight years. The book deals with the social basis of theology, the problem of the particular and the universal in theological discourse, and the bibilical bases of black theology. Must readings.

Lincoln, C. Eric, ed., *The Black Experience in Religion* (Garden City, N.Y.: Anchor Press, 1974).
> A collection of 25 essays on black religious experience in Africa, the Caribbean and the U.S. by a variety of competent authors from each of these worlds. Well done as a quick survey of the field.

Reist, Benjamin A., *Theology in Red, White, and Black* (Philadelphia: Westminster Press, 1975).
> Written by a white systematic theologian, this book contains valuable material and interpretations of native American and black religious experience, and proposes new conditions for theological discourse in this country.

Roberts, J. Deotis, *A Black Political Theology* (Philadelphia: Westminster Press, 1974).
> The second most prolific of the black theologians, Roberts takes a much more conservative, integrationist posture than anyone else writing black theology today. This book is an attempt to outline the dimensions of a black political theology. It raises the questions of such a theology but is not a formulation of the theology itself.

Wilmore, Gayraud, S., *Black Religion and Black Radicalism* (Garden City, N.Y.: Doubleday, 1972).
> Wilmore traces the idea of freedom in the religions of Africa and in black experience on this continent. He is concerned with the religious roots of that idea and its manifestations in both secular and religious experience. Well worth reading.

THE EMERGENCE OF THE VOLUNTARY CHURCH

By W. WIDICK SCHROEDER

The separation of church and state is the most important single socio-cultural factor affecting the shape and style of American religious institutions. This separation has made the principle of religious voluntarism preeminent and has fostered the emergence of the related values of religious pluralism and religious tolerance.

The notions of church-state separation, religious liberty, religious pluralism and religious tolerance have become central core values shared by most Americans. They hold these foundational convictions more fundamentally than they hold most particular religious beliefs. Consequently, the beliefs of those faith communities holding alternative views of church-state relations have been qualified and transformed by the American religious experiment. The predominance of these widely held convictional values in contemporary America has made the voluntary church the predominant form of religious organization in America.

This historic development is traced through selective historical retrieval in the first half of this essay. In the second half the contemporary situation is assessed, and alternative views of "church renewal" are discussed.

THE EUROPEAN AND AMERICAN ANTECEDENTS OF THE VOLUNTARY CHURCH

Human beings differ in the intensity of their involvements in faith communities. Some people are extraordinarily sensitive to the Divine Presence in the world, and they frequently respond to their awareness of the Divine Presence by very substantial involvement in a faith community. Others are moderately and still others marginally involved.

Shifting climates of opinion in the various epochs of Christian history have affected the proportions of the population with high, moderate and low involvement in faith communities in different historical periods, but every epoch has had some people in each group.

In Europe varying religious sensitivities and institutional involvements contributed to the development of "church" and "sect" type faith communities, so astutely analyzed by Ernst Troeltsch some two generations ago. According to Troeltsch, church type faith communities are more inclusive in membership, less demanding of members, less biblically focused, and less egalitarian than sect type faith communities. Sects seek the total involvement and total commitment of their members, and they often accentuate the New Testament model of the church. They minimize the clergy-laity contrast, and they often have egalitarian emphases. They usually contrast more sharply the disparity between the church and the world.

In America, a hybrid institution which is neither a church nor a sect in the European sense has evolved. It is a "voluntary" church, distinguished by the fact that members belong because they **will** to belong. The denomination has become the predominant form of "connectional" institution, relating various "gathered" fellowships.

These summary observations require clarification and elaboration. A selective historical retrieval will facilitate this process.

THE EUROPEAN ANTECEDENTS

Neither Luther nor Calvin envisaged religious liberty in the contemporary American sense. Both sought to substitute their version of an established state church for the Catholic version.

In the sixteenth century, the princes of the small principalities of what is now Germany determined whether a given area would become Protestant or remain Catholic. Their decisions were often shaped as much by political and economic factors as by religious issues.

In the theocracy of Calvin's Geneva the religious liberty of the nonconformist was severely circumscribed. The state stood ready to coerce ·those persons whom the church determined were violating church teaching or practice.

The people associated with the movements subsequently called the "Left Wing of the Reformation" are the precursors of the contemporary voluntary church. They emphasized the primacy of the intentional fellowship, a faith community composed of those whose experiences had led them to form churches in which discipline under God, the authority of Scripture, right belief and right conduct were central.

In the German speaking portion of the Reformation Anabaptists such as the Mennonites were representative of the intentional fellowship; in the English speaking world, various Baptist bodies related to the Calvinistic tradition were representative. These groups had markedly different views of church-world relations. Mennonites sought to withdraw from worldly entanglements, and most Baptists sought to influence public policy. In spite of these differences, they both believed the gathered fellowship was the proper type of faith community.

The religious organization of the American colonies was shaped by the expectations of the early English settlers. Seventeenth century English Puritan-Anglican struggles spilled over into the colonies, for Puritans predominated in New England and Anglicans predominated in the South.

As was the case with sixteenth century Lutherans and Calvinists, neither Puritans nor Anglicans sought to disestablish the church. They disagreed on the type of church to be established, but they affirmed the general principle of establishment **per se.** The notions of religious liberty and a pluralism of fellowships were affirmed in principle only in Rhode Island and Pennsylvania.

As time passed, the colonies became more and more heterogeneous religiously, for settlers coming from various parts of Europe with different established churches became more numerous in all of the colonies. This social reality which encouraged disestablishment was accentuated by cultural and political developments in the eighteenth century.

Deistic modes of thought emerging in the Enlightenment fostered the ideas of religious pluralism, voluntarism, and tolerance, complementing the Quaker and Baptist views. The sectarian wars that had plagued Europe made an impact on American leadership, and most American political leaders were very anxious to avoid the religious wars that had devasted parts of Europe.

Thus, the embryonic secularity of Deism, the piety of some Christian bodies, and the practicality of American political leadership contributed to the emergence of the doctrine of the separation of church and state. The Congress of the new republic affirmed this doctrine by adopting the First Amendment of the Constitution, guaranteeing religious liberty. The Supreme Court subsequently ruled that the First Amendment applied only to the Federal Government, but its suasive power was considerable. In 1833, Massachusetts, the last state to have an established church, disestablished it. The American religious experiment, informed by piety and practicality, was fully launched.

FROM WASHINGTON TO LINCOLN: A PROTESTANT PLURALISM

In the early days of the Republic the nation was nominally Protestant in overwhelming proportions. In 1790 there were only 40,000 Catholics and at most a few thousand Jews in a population of almost 4,000,000.

Fewer than five percent of that population belonged to a church, so the field was ripe for intensive evangelism. The revivalistic activities in the latter half of the eighteenth century and the first half of the nineteenth century were set in the context of this dual situation — a very low proportion of the population associated with the churches and an evolving disestablishment. If the churches of America were to survive, they had to have more members. America's religious leaders — often with more evangelical zeal than theological perspicacity — set about this recruitment task with vigor and enthusiasm.

Under the dual influences of evanglism and church-state separation the pluralism of Protestantism caused by the migration of people affiliated with different Protestant bodies in Europe was augmented by the proliferation of indigenous groups in the nineteenth century. The extraordinarily large number of denominations in America is an outgrowth of these factors.

The seventeenth century pattern of Puritan migration to the New England colonies and of Anglican migration to the Southern colonies was noted earlier. The impact of those migrations was still observable in the nineteenth century. The unique character of Southern religion in America is a result of the blending of earlier Anglican influences with the biblicism and revivalism of the eighteenth and nineteenth centuries. The medieval social theory so predominant among seventeenth century Anglican divines who migrated from England to Virginia and some of the other Southern colonies contributed greatly to the quasi-feudal character of the Old South. The aristocracy, the style of chivalry, the elevated status of women, and the interpretation of slavery as a white man's burden were rooted in this conservative Anglican tradition. Formal involvement in the Anglican Church was very low in the latter part of the eighteenth century, and the South was ripe for the evangelism and the biblically informed revivalism that became firmly entrenched in this region. Despite this overlay, the early Anglican "layer" contributed substantially to the emergence of a distinctive style of Christianity in this region.

The Puritan influence was widespread in the North and the West in the first half of the nineteenth century and exacerbated regional conflicts. It is possible to trace some of the roots of the Civil War to the contrasting beliefs of the seventeenth century Puritan and Anglican immigrants — contrasts which had produced a Civil War in seventeenth century England.

During this epoch, the idea of religious disestablishment was firmly embodied in the American experiment. The public school was evolving to a central position in American education and the "Sunday School," a typically American enterprise integrally related to the voluntary church, was taking form.

The overwhelming Protestant character of the country was modified somewhat during this time. The number of Catholic immigrants increased, particularly in the latter part of the period, for the potato famine in Ireland and the European political unrest in 1848 encouraged more Catholics to immigrate.

FROM LINCOLN TO WILSON: URBANIZATION, INDUSTRIALIZATION, AND THE EMERGENCE OF A MULTI-FAITH PLURALISM

In the post-Civil War epoch the United States was transformed from a predominantly rural, agrarian and overwhelmingly Protestant country to an urban, industrial, and less predominantly Protestant country. The tremendous mass migrations in this period, particularly from 1885-1915, altered markedly the ethnic and religious composition of the nation. Between 1880 and 1920 almost 25,000,000 immigrants settled in this nation, and the proportion of Catholics in the population increased dramatically.

Catholics coming from Southern and Eastern Europe knew almost nothing of religious liberty, religious pluralism, religious tolerance and church-state separation. They developed an extensive parochial school system and numerous Catholic welfare institutions during this time, for they sought to develop religious institutions similar to the ones they had known in their homelands.

The Jewish population of America increased substantially during this time, for they participated in the migrations from both Northern and Eastern Europe. They still remained a small proportion of the American population (less than three percent), but their actual number increased markedly.

The earlier consensus attained on church-state separation was shaken but not shattered during this epoch. Subject to various forms of persecution at the hands of both Catholics and Protestants in Europe, the Jewish immigrants enthusiastically affirmed the principle of church-state separation. Catholic affirmation was more restrained and less enthusiastic, for many Catholic immigrants came from areas of Europe in which Catholicism was the predominant religion and in which the church enjoyed special privileges and support from the state. These contrasting interpretations of church-state relations created difficulties, compounded by the fact that many of these immigrants came from parts of Europe with monarchical or aristocratic govenments and knew little or nothing about a democratic form of government. Crowding into the burgeoning industrial cities of the North, they often became urban villagers, seeking to claim some turf as their own. In this context, the Statue of Liberty took on major symbolic significance, and the "melting-pot" theory of culturalization became popular.

During this period the black church in America became a visible social institution. There were a few black churches among free blacks in the an-

27

tebellum period, but the end of slavery saw the tremendous expansion of black churches in the South. The shape and style of the black church was affected not only by the commingling of Anglican and evangelical influences in the South but also by the character of the black experience in America. The black church emerged as an inclusive social institution, dealing not only with religious matters but also with social, economic, and political issues.

THE PREEMINENCE OF THE VOLUNTARY CHURCH IN TWENTIETH CENTURY AMERICA

Within the framework of religious voluntarism, three major faith communities have evolved: Protestant, Catholic, Jewish. Because of different early histories and the persistence of segregation, American Protestantism divided into predominantly white denominations and predominantly black denominations. Thus, the cultural and social realities of the American experience have differentiated white Protestantism from black Protestantism, giving rise to four major faith communities.

The contemporary voluntary church differs markedly in one respect from the intentional fellowships of the Reformation epoch discussed previously. The voluntary church does not demand that its members affirm the strong emphases on right discipline under God, the authority of Scripture, right belief and right conduct, emphases characteristic of the "Believers' Church" of the Reformation era. It accepts almost anyone who chooses to belong. Intentional fellowships do exist, but they incorporate fewer people than do the voluntary churches.

Because the separation of church and state precludes the use of tax money for the support of faith communities, American clergy in the voluntary church have had to develop more innovative and often more imaginative programs than their European counterparts. The fund-raising aspects of bake sales, auctions, and many faith community sponsored programs reflect the practicality and activism of the voluntary church.

The paucity of significant anti-clericalism in the United States is also related to the voluntary church, for no faith community has been able to impose directly its teachings in the public realm. Most members in the voluntary church prefer priestly activities to prophetic ones. At the cultural level, the separation of church and state has limited the power of the church to address public issues. At the personal level, members of the voluntary church do not want undue internal conflict; they prefer adjustive, integrative styles of leadership to challenging and disintegrative ones. Leaders may engage in prophetic activity from time to time, provided they engage predominantly in priestly activities.

Local professionals are under substantial pressure to conform to lay expectations, for lay people in every tradition are free to dissociate themselves from their faith community if they will to do so. In some traditions they may dismiss leaders if the contrast in clergy-lay expectations become inordinate. In all traditions, lay people make things difficult for clergy with whom they have substantial disagreement.

THE MAJOR FAITH COMMUNITIES IN CONTEMPORARY AMERICA: WHITE PROTESTANT, BLACK PROTESTANT, CATHOLIC AND JEWISH

Four major faith communities have evolved in the context of the American religious experiment: white Protestant, black Protestant, Catholic, and Jewish. Protestantism is the majority religion, and Judaism is a small minority. Church membership data are not very reliable, but the best estimates indicate a relatively steady increase in the proportion of the American people affiliated with a faith community from the time of the founding of the country until the late 1950s, at which time between 65 and 70 percent of American adults were affiliated with a religious institution. Since then a modest decline in the proportion of adults belonging to churches has taken place.

About 65 to 70 percent of Americans belonging to religious institutions belong to Protestant churches, about 25 to 30 percent belong to Catholic churches, and about two or three percent belong to Jewish synagogues. Of the 70 to 75 million Protestant church members, some 10 to 12 million are black.

The principles of organization and authority differ within and between these faith communities. The impact of the American religious experiment on these principles needs to be considered.

VOLUNTARISM, PRINCIPLES OF ORGANIZATION, AND AUTHORITY IN THE MAJOR FAITH COMMUNITIES

As noted earlier, the principle of church-state separation and the concomitant principles of religious liberty, religious tolerance, and religious pluralism undergird the American religious experiment. These principles are more foundational for the vast majority of Americans today than are the principles of any particular religious tradition. As a consequence, the understanding of faith communities as "gathered fellowships" has become the normative understanding among most Americans. As noted earlier, relatively few highly intentional religious fellowships exist in contemporary America; most Protestant faith communities and the Catholic Church have been transformed or are being transformed into predominantly voluntary churches.

There is one major historical difference between most Protestant faith communities and Catholicism. Most Protestant bodies have had two or three centuries to accommodate themselves to the American religious experiment. By contrast the Catholic Church has had only three generations, for the flood of Catholic immigrants between 1885 and 1915 knew nothing of the emergence of the American religious experiment and of the foundational values embodied in it.

This historical difference is compounded by ecclesiastical and doctrinal contrasts, for the predominant principle of organization has differed in the faith communities. In American Protestantism as a whole, the **congregational** principle of the primacy of the local congregation has predominated. Episcopal and Presbyterian principles of organization are extant, but they are substantially qualified and modified by the congregational principle. As noted earlier, the congregational principle is reinforced by the principle of voluntarism embodied in general American cultural values. Both lay people and clergy can move from one of the more than 250 Protestant denominations to another without renouncing their Protestant faith identity, providing substantial internal diversity and opportunities for lay and clergy self-selection.

In Protestantism, the question of authority centers on the authority of Scripture. Some persons and groups think it is the unequivocal locus for matters of faith and order; others think it is not. Among the former group, conflict emerges about alternative interpretations of Scripture and differing implications to be drawn from it. Among the latter, internal differences emerge, for no consensus about the locus of authority or the shape of faith and order exists.

In Catholicism, a **cultic** principle of organization has been predominant. A specially designated, hierarchically organized body of priests has set policy, prescribed doctrines, and administered rites for the laity. The multiplicity of Catholic religious orders and the distinction between secular and religious priests have provided some internal diversity within Catholicism, but Catholic emphases on "true" doctrine and a hierarchial system of authority culminating in the authority of the Pope have substantially limited the extent of internal diversity. A Catholic cannot move from one subcommunity to another and retain his basic Catholic faith identity in the same way a Protestant can.

The inner turmoil currently manifest in American Catholicism, which is substantially greater than in Protestantism or Judaism, is a result of the recent widespead affirmation of the voluntaristic principle by Catholic clergy and laity. The increased emphasis on the laity since Vatican II coheres with the principle of voluntarism. The development of various structures to facilitate lay involvement in the decision making processes within the American Catholic Church in the past decade or two is also in tune with the principles informing the American religious experiment. In Catholicism, the question of authority centers on the authority of the tradition. Laity-laity, clergy-clergy, and laity-clergy conflicts about the degree of voluntarism compatible with Catholicism and about the locus of authority within the church are commonplace.

In Judaism, a **communal** principle of organization is predominant, for the Jewish religious community is inextricably intertwined with the history of the Jewish people. Jews may move from one of the three sub-communities to another without renouncing their basic Jewishness. In addition to the religious subgroups numerous "secular" Jewish agencies exist. Since many American Jews have great difficulty affirming the "religious" side of their historic community, these "secular" agencies also serve as a way for Jews to retain Jewish social identity on the context of their detachment from synagogues. The communal principle of organization coheres with a congregational principle, so the voluntarism of the American religious experiment was readily compatible with the Jewish experience. In Judaism the question of authority centers around the question of the authority of the Jewish community. The debate is multi-faceted, since the relation of the "religious" community to the "historic" community and the authority of the historic community are intertwined issues.

Previously it was noted that the earlier "Believers' Church" emphasized discipline under God, the authority of Scripture, right belief, and right conduct. The members of the voluntary church in contemporary America do not uniformly affirm these emphases, and the implications of this situation warrant special consideration.

THE VOLUNTARY CHURCH AND LEVELS OF INTENTIONALITY

In the voluntary church, which all evidence indicates is the preeminent form of the church in contemporary America, members belong because they **will** to belong. Strict membership criteria are rare, and any person who wants to belong to a church will have no difficulty in finding one which will be happy to have him. Only among some "Believers' Churches" do strict covenants and membership criteria exist, and these communities are distinguished by their paucity.

In most of the Protestant churches of the major denominations, such as the American Baptist Churches in the USA, Episcopal Church, the Lutheran Church in America, the United Church of Christ, the United Methodist Church, and the United Presbyterian Church, and in Catholicism, people with widely varying levels of intentionality and commitment coexist in the same congregations. A few members (usually less than ten percent) are highly involved and deeply committed to their church; many (usually about one-half to two-thirds) have a significant measure of commitment; some (usually about one-quarter) are marginally involved, and a few (usually about ten percent) are merely on the membership roll. Since the level of one's commitment and the **substance** of one's commitment may differ, the members in a given congregation whose levels of commitment are high may differ in the substance of their commitments. In more evangelical groups, such as churches in the Southern Baptist Convention and the Lutheran Church-Missouri Synod, the level of intentionality is higher than in the previously cited denominations, but these denominations also have substantial proportions of marginal and dormant members. In Judaism the same general patterns prevail, except that the proportions of marginal and dormant members are higher than in Catholicism or Protestantism. People are free to "shop" for an appropriate religious institution in Protestantism and Judaism. Catholics are encouraged to attend the church in their geographical parish, but in recent decades more of them are seeking a church that fits their religious and social style. Most people will to belong to religious institutions with people of similar social status and ethnicity, so particular congregations tend to have members in about the same social status and tend to be ethnically homogeneous.

The voluntary church places primacy on the local congregation. Those denominations with episcopal or presbyterian polities are connectional, and are not as directly subject to the will of local congregations as are denominations with a congregational polity, but in America they must also pay considerable attention to the expectations and interests of local congregations. Local lay people expect to be consulted in major decisions; and they expect to have some voice in the decision making process, regardless of the form of church government prevailing in their denomination. They are willing to listen to their leader's views on faith and morals, but they reserve the right to make up their own minds.

The widely varying levels of participation, theological understanding and spiritual maturity among the members of the voluntary church in America place very special demands upon religious leaders. Their responses depend upon their theories of religious leadership and their theological interpretations of this situation.

Interpretations of the situation and strategies for "church renewal" abound. It is fitting to conclude this essay with a brief discussion of alternative strategies for "church renewal."

THE VOLUNTARY CHURCH AND STRATEGIES FOR "CHURCH RENEWAL"

The core values informing the lives of most Americans emerge from a variety of sources. The religions of America discussed here are one source of meaning. The public faith of America, including the religion of America (a complex faith incorporating belief in separation of church and state, religious liberty, religious pluralism and religious tolerance and other motifs not discussed here), technical rationalism and secular humanism, are another source of meaning. Taken together they constitute a blending of piety and practicality shared unevenly and in a less than fully coherent way by most Americans.

Participants in the voluntary church affirm many aspects of the public faith of America, resulting in complex and subtle transformations of their historic faith communities. One's evaluation of this situation and one's suggested responses to it will be guided by his views on the following issues: the nature of "authentic" religion; the relation between "authentic" religion, other religions, and human culture; the relation between love, justice, and forms of social organization; and the extent of the harmony of life with life possible under the conditions of existence. These issues cannot be elaborated adequately here, but some observations about the way in which theological understanding informs some of the diverse strategies for "church renewal" can be made.

Persons preferring the intentional fellowship inevitably criticize the voluntary church and offer various strategies to intensify the depth of commitment of church members. They often lament the loss of discipline characteristic of earlier intentional fellowships and seek to restore it. Since only a fraction of the members of the typical voluntary church respond to such "renewal" efforts by professional leadership, some self-conscious "elites" emerge who have different visions of the nature of the church than most of the participants. Such contrasting views not infrequently lead to internal struggles within congregations, for not all members share either the style or substance of the understandings being advocated by the "renewalists."

Some persons seeking the restoration of intentional communities are informed by kerygmatic styles of theology. Consequently, they focus attention on the Bible and/or facets of the tradition (often the early church). They seek to cultivate groups engaged in Bible study in the context of reflection on current experience. Others are informed by apologetic styles of theology. They also cultivate small groups, but they are more apt to be informed by humanistic psychology and other contemporary modes of thought. Persons seeking the restoration of the intentional fellowship entertain differing views of the church's involvement in politics. Some seek direct involvement in the political sphere, but others accentuate the need for substantial distance or withdrawal from politics.

Persons whose views on the nature of the church permit them to accept the reality of the voluntary church with more equanimity than more sectarian protagonists offer more moderate and balanced suggestions for "church renewal." Because "institutional maintainence" is not such a negative word for them, they are likely to be more supportive of activities sustaining existing enterprises. Since only the most insensitive do not see the need for innovation and for opportunities to cultivate deeper theological understanding and spiritual maturation, such persons support some innovative and "renewing" efforts. Those are set, however, in the context of a more sympathetic interpretation of the current situation.

The vision of the religious professional as a "pastoral director," "a facilitator," and/or an "enabler" is compatible with this latter view. Accepting members with markedly different degrees of commitment and spiritual maturation, protagonists of this perspective are able to foster and to support the multiple programs of worship, education and social activities typical of the voluntary church.

Professionals willing to commit themselves to a process of consensus formation in a faith community, seeking to sustain a spiritual and moral community bearing witness to the Divine Presence in human life and desiring a limited pluralism in style and substance can serve the voluntary church with integrity. They know full well their efforts will be fragmentary, imperfect, and ambivalent, but they believe the positive aspects of the voluntary church justify these efforts. Informed by a sense of cause, a sense of proportion, and a sense of responsibility, such professional leadership may legitimately hope to enhance human life and to contribute to the Divine Life.

NOTES:

Much of the material summarized in this essay is elaborated and documented in detail in W. Widick Schroeder, Victor Obenhaus, Larry A. Jones, and Thomas Sweetser, *Suburban Religion: Churches and Synagogues in the American Experience* (Chicago, 1974). In the last chapter of the volume, the author of this essay offers a sympathetic constructive interpretation of the voluntary church. Thomas P. Sweetser's *The Catholic Parish: Shifting Membership in a Changing Church* (Chicago, 1974) focuses on the Catholic data reported in the preceeding citation.

Sydney E. Ahlstrom's *A Religious History of the American People* (New Haven, 1972) is an encyclopedic treatment of American religious history. Martin E. Marty's *Righteous Empire: The Protestant Experience in America* (New York, 1970) emphasizes the Puritan influence in America. Sydney Mead's *The Lively Experiment: The Shaping of Christianity in America* (New York, 1963) focuses of religious liberty and the physical fact of the "frontier" in interpreting Christianity in America.

Winthrop Hudson's *American Protestantism* (Chicago, 1961), John Tracy Ellis' *American Catholicism* (Chicago, 1956) and Nathan Glazer's *American Judaism* (Chicago, 1972) are useful surveys of the histories of these three faith communities in America. E. Franklin Frazier's *The Negro Church in America* (New York, 1963) and Joseph Washington's *Black Religion: The Negro and Christianity in the United States* (Boston, 1964) are helpful analyses of the black church in America.

Useful sociological studies of contemporary American religion include: Will Herberg, *Protestant, Catholic, Jew* (New York, 1955); Gerhard Lenski, *The Religious Factor* (New York,

1961); Rodney Stark and Charles Y. Glock, *American Piety: The Nature of Religious Commitment* (Berkeley, 1968); and Martin E. Marty, Stuart E. Rosenberg and Andrew M. Greeley, *What Do We Believe? The Stance of Religion in America* (New York, 1968).

Franklin H. Littell's *From State Church to Pluralism* (Garden City, 1962) combines historical analysis with an appeal for church renewal of the kerygmatic intentional community type. Philip and Phoebe Anderson elaborate their views of church renewal of an apologetic intentional community type in *The House Church* (Nashville, 1975).

The following volumes deal with "church renewal" from the perspective of the voluntary church: H. Richard Niebuhr, *The Purpose of the Church and Its Ministry* (New York, 1956); James Gustafson, *Treasure in Earthen Vessels* (New York, 1961); James Dittes, *The Church in the Way* (New York, 1967); and James Nelson, *Moral Nexus* (Philadelphia, 1971).

WHERE TWO OR THREE ARE GATHERED TOGETHER: DENOMINATIONALISM AND THE ROLE OF WOMEN

By BARBARA BROWN ZIKMUND

American religious leaders have often been aplogetic and negative about the story of religion in America. Although our history has not been dotted with many great theological leaders, it is important for us to understand the unique features of American religious life. Where two or three have gathered together to call upon the Lord, the result has been the denomination — a uniquely American development.

My colleague Widick Schroeder has described the emergence and characteristics of the voluntary church in another essay. My purpose is to explore denominational theory and its relationship to the situation of the laity within American religious life. I also want to examine the implications of this tradition for contemporary understandings of ministry. I am particularly concerned that the past and present circumstances of women not be overlooked.

DENOMINATIONALISM

Church historians have often described the organizational circumstances of the church in terms of Ernst Troeltsch's typology of "church" and "sect." Without going into detail, the major distinctions classically drawn between the church and the sect have been over issues of inclusiveness, relationship to civil authorities, and the type of commitment demanded of members. In continental Europe, churches and sectarian groups had no concept of religious pluralism. If any group could dominate an area and impose uniformity, this was generally considered appropriate. Those who did not agree with the religious group in power were expected to change or move elsewhere.

The concept of denominationalism comes out of the eighteenth century Evangelical Revival in England. It finds full expression and development in American history. Consequently it is appropriate to quote John Wesley, who felt bound to all Christians by the "common principles of Christianity." Wesley renounced and abhored being set apart from Christians "of whatever denomination." By that term Wesley paid homage to a doctrine of the church which refused to equate the true church with particular ecclesiastical structures. This was a doctrine of the church uniquely appropriate to the American scene.

Denominationalism is also based upon a view of the church in keeping with the theology and experience of the Protestant Reformation. The admonitions of Luther and Calvin that no particular church form and practice should become an idolatrous object of worship, provided a climate for diversity. In Anglo-American experience historical circumstances allowed Protestant Christians to develop a denominational theory which denied the exclusivistic characteristics of both the "church" and the "sect." Indeed, American piety in pushing the Protestant principle to its limit in defining the church, and American practicality in nurturing an ecclesiology accommodating to religious diversity have combined to produce the denomination.

The denomination is an ecclesiastical group co-existing with other groups in a tolerant and free environment. Whereas both the church and the sect make authoritative and exclusivistic claims, the denomination is apologetic in its stance. No denomination claims to represent the total church. No denomination claims that all other churches are false. The Puritan Independents argued for necessary diversity in order to express the unity of the faith. Each denomination is a different "mode" of expression **needed** to proclaim the oneness of Christ.

The "sect" claims an exclusive and narrow path to salvation. Followers believe that they have the only way, the true vision. The "church" claims an authoritative and broadly based way. Uniformity of faith and order assure followers that theirs is the correct stance (at least for that time and place). The denomination claims that human fraility and finitude inevitably produce diversity in Christian practice. Believers will differ in judgment about the life and character of the church. That is to be expected. Furthermore, these differences are important and should be allowed expression. Every Christian is under obligation to practice according to personal conviction. To do otherwise is to allow human judgment to become the Lord of one's conscience.

Denominationalism does not despair at this pluralism. Rather, it recognizes that differences of opinion, honestly held, can produce discussion leading to a fuller understanding of God's truth. The fact of separation does not constitute schism. Christians may be divided at many points, but the unity of Christ transcends the variety. Ecclesiastical uniformity is secondary to the oneness of God in Christ.

Denominational humility is the obvious result of such a theory. Since no church practice, polity or principle expresses final unambiguous truth, the true Church of Christ can never be fully represented by any single ecclesiastical structure. Each group, therefore, strives to do its best, and all structures serve as constant correctives to the pretensions which tempt human organizations. In theory, at least, denominationalism always tempers its piety with theological humility as well as practicality. In the American religious experiment the tension between basic theological unity and practical diversity has been upheld for over two hundred years.

At times, however, although denominational theory became a means of enabling major Protestant groups to cooperate for the achievement of common ends, it also has allowed classic Christian concerns to be compromised in ecumenical enthusiasm. As Winthrop Hudson has put it, the great temptation has been to transform denominationalism from a means of expressing unity into a means of securing unity. In our openness to others, American chruches have sometimes reduced the core of commonly held beliefs which inform practice to a vague "lowest common denominator." Without casting further judgment upon later developments, suffice it to say that the voluntary chruch in America finds its theoretical heritage in the eighteenth century case for denominationalism. This religious stance has had particular ramifications on the character of the laity in American churches.

AMERICAN DENOMINATIONALISM AND THE LAITY

From the very beginning of American colonial church life, the situation of the laity was different. Whereas most of the early colonists were of British stock, a certain form of self-selection operated to make colonial religion quite different on this side of the Atlantic ocean. For although the new settlers wished to know themselves as British subjects in every way, the fact that the more intentional, daring and less entrenched citizen chose to come to the New World produced an independent and self-confident colonial populace. Furthermore, the personal risk and pride invested in maintaining colonial life tended to perpetuate personal qualities of singular strength.

It appears, therefore, that a certain type of person chose to come to this land. And furthermore, that the character of life in the colonies called for innovation and adjustment significantly freed from past practices. This development combined with emerging denominational theory to create a new type of church on the American scene.

Although the colonial church in New England and the Southern colonies was patterned formally after the establishment model, the character of these churches was radically changed long before final disestablishment in the early nineteenth century. The crucial development in colonial religion focused upon the role of the laity.

Puritanism was a lay centered movement, and English Separatism also was radically concerned for the laity. In New England the commitment to local congregational autonomy gave a select group of lay members significant control over the churches. Even in the Anglican parishes of Virginia the power of the laity was unusually strong. Each parish was governed by a Vestry. Although churches received clergy as appointed by the episcopacy, it was not unusual for a Virginia vestry to refuse to present a minister to the Royal Governor for induction if they had any reservations about him. Fully trained Anglican leaders were scarce in the colonies, and those that served were held accountable to the laity in very direct ways. Americans were so wary of episcopal interference that a resident episcopacy in the Anglican churches was not established on this side of the Atlantic until after 1789.

Colonial religion and church membership was initially elitist. That is, only a small minority of the population belonged to or related to the churches in any way. The impact of the first Great Awakening, which swept the colonies in the 1740s and 1750s, was to draw more people into the churches. The Great Awakening, however, was fanned by itinerant revivalists and characterized by emotionalism. It had the effect of further undercutting clerical leadership and power. Ecclesiastical tradition, form and order were always judged secondary when considered alongside the work of the spirit in revivalism. Furthermore, the Great Awakening generated tremendous lay enthusiasm about the church, producing the high lay commitment to church life that has characterized American Christianity for at least 200 years.

The strong role of the laity in American churches was also stimulated by the emerging concept of separation of church and state grounded in denominational theory. If no particular church could claim an authoritative or exclusive path to salvation, there was no logic to an established church. Indeed a single church would deny the people the benefits of pluralism. Even when people did not accept this logic, the proliferating numbers of religious groups soon forged a practical principle of church-state separation, which in turn stimulated strong lay involvement.

Church-state separation forced church members to take responsibility for all facets of church life. Taxes were not available to fund buildings or pay salaries. The people had to commit time and money to have a church. And, as with all buyers, they wanted a reasonable say in what they were purchasing. The voluntary church has been a significant reason for the high lay involvement in American churches. It has stimulated lay interest, and has limited clerical prerogatives. Not only have members in a voluntary church been more involved, the clergy have also been less authoritarian. Unable to function beyond the claim of lay judgment, American ministers have pioneered in collaborative and enabling styles of ministry. Until very recently the Protestant ministry in America enjoyed a "folk esteem" rather than a "professional image."

One other factor must be mentioned to complete the picture, that is the importance of the frontier environment in stimulating strong lay participation. While scholars may debate the details, it is a well accepted fact that much of American history has been influenced by the pervading presence of a frontier. Spreading westward with each succeeding generation, the frontier provided an area of minimal restraint, increased individualism and democratic involvement. For the churches, the frontier was dominated by the laity.

The institutional church sparked by the Protestant Reformation was theologically and organizationally quite adaptable to frontier conditions. On the one hand the reformers' emphasis upon the "priesthood of all believers" encouraged democratic churches. Protestant Americans were skeptical about authority in any form. They were quick to develop political, theological and ecclesiastical independence appropriate to frontier life. On the other hand, groups from the free church tradition of the radical reformation found in the American frontier a hospitable habitat. Many settlers, already committed to strong lay participation, came to this land and were fruitful and multiplied. Either way, frontier circumstances clearly caused even the most traditionally based groups, such as the Methodists, to adjust. Although its government and heritage is rooted in Anglican understandings of clergy and laity, Methodism thrived on the frontier. Trained clergy were not available and Methodism turned to lay preachers and class leaders for leadership. Methodist circuit riders traveled hundreds of miles, leaving laity in charge of congregations, for months at a time. Methodism further appealed to frontier thinking with its modified Arminian gospel that promised grace and universal salvation. Massive camp meetings allowed revivalists, who were usually uneducated lay persons in all but name, to become spiritual guides for many converts. The extent of lay involvement in frontier church life cannot be exaggerated.

The frontier also spawned indigenous American denominations that were consciously committed to the laity. The Disciples of Christ are a good example. Thomas and Alexander Campbell, who spearheaded much of the movement to form this denomination, were insistent that laity had the right to teach, preach and administer the sacraments. The minister in the Disciples tradition is functionally set apart by one congregation to service its needs. If a minister leaves that group, he or she has no particular office or privileges, unless another congregation similarly designates the person. The final power of the church is always in the hands of the congregation.

Even some of the more sectarian or unusual communitarian religious groups witness to the importance of the laity. The Shakers, the Quakers, the Mormons and the Adventists all give the laity a strong voice. In some cases there is no clerical group at all; in other cases all members of the group constitute a "priesthood." Certainly the class lines and distinctions between a priestly group and the believers became particularly hard to maintain on the American frontier.

Denominational theory was rooted in English experience of the eighteenth century. American denominationalism, however, expanded the logic of organizational humility, which argued that no one church could consider itself **the** true church, to make a case for lay power in the churches. Not only was one church no better than another, the clergy were no better than the laity. The resulting practice in American church experience was denominational diversity and strong lay participation.

INTERDENOMINATIONAL LAY MOVEMENTS

Given this diversity and participation, the nineteenth century in America was characterized by many interdenominational movements promoted by church members. American practicality did not let the labels get in the way if there was a task to be done or a problem to be solved. American piety often looked beyond the denominations to deal with issues. .

Certainly the best example of interdenominational cooperation can be seen in the anti-slavery movement. Throughout the North in the years leading up to the civil conflict, church people organized societies and worked for gradual colonization or immediate abolition. Many laymen and women were convinced that their Christian commitment was violated by slavery and they organized the underground railway to help the runaway slave. Even when denominational organizations and clerical leadership were not supportive, courageous lay persons participated in the great drive to free their Black brothers and sisters.

Another example of lay commitment is seen in the development of the Sunday school movement. From their beginnings the Sunday schools were started, supervised and supported by lay persons — often against clergy opposition. In the early nineteenth century as public education became more secular, church people joined Sunday school unions to promote religious instruction. It was only after the 1820s, when the churches began incorporating Sunday schools into regular programs, that the clergy became involved. Indeed, to this day the Sunday schools continue to bring lay persons together as they struggle to nurture children in the faith.

41

Youth movements and young adult organizations are another arena where strong ecumenical lay activity is traditional. The founding of the YMCA (Young Men's Christian Association) in 1844 in London was particularly important for America. From the beginning it considered itself a voluntary lay movement auxiliary to the churches, but without affiliation with any denomination. It spread quickly in America and eventually spawned the Student Volunteer Movement. After the YWCA was founded, lay persons of both sexes turned to the "Y" for programs designed to develop the spiritual, mental and physical capacities of individuals. It is important to remember that the "Y" stands because of the commitment of Christian lay people.

In 1881 another important group called the Young People's Society of Christian Endeavor was founded. Although Christian Endeavor groups met in churches, the organization was lay controlled and interdenominational. Many Americans during the early twentieth century made their first commitment to Christianity in the Christian Endeavor society, not through denominational church membership.

Of course the entire missionary outreach activity of major nineteenth century Protestant denominations, such as the Congregationalists and the Presbyterians, was interdenominational and lay controlled. In 1810 the American Board of Commissioners for Foreign Missions was founded by some graduating theological students. Interdenominational from the start, the American Board soon supported many committed missionaries all over the world. The story of the American Home Missionary Society is similar. Organized in 1826, the society became the most important single home missionary agency among American Protestants before the Civil War. In both of these organizations lay participation, lay policy making, lay service and lay support were fundamental to their growth and success.

And finally, no survey of lay activity in the churches can be complete without some word about temperance. Although initially temperance supporters were committed to moderation in the use of alcoholic drink, "temperance" came to mean total abstinence after 1800 in America. The American Temperance Society was founded in 1826. It promoted an abstinence pledge and worked for legal prohibition. In 1869 the Prohibition Party politicized the movement, but the founding of the Women's Christian Temperance Union in 1874 and the Anti-Saloon League in 1893 kept the movement alive in the churches. Methodism in particular was strongly associated with the temperance cause. In all cases the commitment of Christian lay people to the principle of temperance accounts for its political success in 1920.

It is possible to say, therefore, that American denominationalism not only upheld the finitude of every church organization, it also produced a laity confident of its capacity to solve problems. In the nineteenth century, particularly, this confidence spilled across denominational lines to produce a number of interdenominational lay movements. The anti-slavery crusade, the Sunday school movement, non-sectarian youth associations such as the "Y", various missionary boards, and the temperance movement all developed because of lay conviction and effort.

To this point in this paper, I have studiously avoided speaking specifically about laymen or laywomen. It is important, however, to point out that this tremendous nineteenth century expansion of lay energy in and beyond the churches was closely related to the circumstances of women. Where two or three have gathered together in the history of American Protestantism, many of these church people have been women. Thus, to speak about the role of the laity in abolition, Sunday schools, youth organizations, missionary work and temperance is to speak clearly about women: Women such as Sarah and Angelina Grimké (abolitionists), Caroline Roberts (YWCA founder), Clara Swain (missionary doctor), Frances Willard (WCTU leader) and hundreds of others whose names will never be known.

Any listing of ministerial and official church leadership in American Protestantism is virtually dominated by males. American churches have enjoyed strong and progressive ministers; this cannot be denied. Yet very few of these ministers or church leaders have ever been female. To this day the Christian ministry remains one of the last strongholds of male expectation.

It is not out of order, therefore, to argue that the strength of American denominationalism in the laity is in actual fact a strength grounded in the contributions of women. Women who could not find official, ministerial or formal positions from which to lead the churches did what women have always done — they used other more indirect ways to translate their concerns into action. Women created women's organizations, took leadership positions in general benevolence societies, taught Sunday schools, became missionaries, and campaigned for temperance. Actively involved and concerned women did not let petty denominational divisions or male dominance in the churches limit their witness for the gospel — at least not in the nineteenth century.

THE CONTEMPORARY PROBLEM

In the twentieth century the story of strong lay activity and inspiring women is left behind. Pioneer and frontier churches have become mature social organizations functioning with some of the characteristics of established institutions. As the churches have developed expensive organized programs, church leadership has become more and more "professionalized." National denominational bureaucracies have grown tremendously in recent years. The result is that the clergyman (formal leadership of the churches is still almost exclusively male) is now a trained specialist in religion. While in some ways this professionalization is appropriate and necessary in our complicated technological society, in other ways it is destroying the vitality of American church life.

The problem is that as the churches become more and more professional in structure and personnel, the laity are less and less valued — except as means for carrying out professionally planned programs. The lay person, usually a woman, is a "helper" to the specialist. From the local churches up to the national denominational boards, synods, and assemblies, one has the feeling that the professional staff is calling the plays and the laity is being ignored, if not used. It is a rare decision making situation that the laity do not acquiesce to the "better judgment" of the professionals.

The development of specialized ministries has increased this tendency. Christian education, counseling, evangelism, recreation, and church administration are now recognized specialities. Even when unordained persons are employed in one of these areas, this "clericalized laity" intimidates and paralyzses the average church member. Twentieth century "ordinary" lay persons are usually tempted to leave the planning and substantive work of the churches to the professionals, while they run bazaars, church dinners and car washes to raise money to hire more professionals. No wonder many women are fed up with "church work."

There have been several responses to the "professionalization" of mainline Protestantism in the twentieth century. First there are those who have adjusted their concept of church membership to that of necessary servanthood under the supervision and direction of religious specialists. It is no accident that the post-World War II period of church growth was also the period of the so-called "Feminine Mystique." Women focused their talents and energies on helping husbands and male ministers keep the family and churches alive. For some women this was a period of satisfied fulfullment. But as the appeal of the mystique lost its hold in the 1960s, so too, the helper role of women in the churches began to cloy.

Another very different type of response to "professionalization" can be seen in the proliferation of new denominations and evangelical churches. Reacting against the "religious country club" mentality which characterizes many large twentieth century congregations and the distant programming of denominational officials, many persons have started or joined churches committed to "old-fashioned religion." By this they mean a church concerned with faith and worship, a church where everyone takes an active role in policy development based upon the Bible, a church that does not need a minister with formal schooling and book learning, a church where laity and clergy wait upon the Lord together.

Many of these churches stand clearly in a nineteenth century evangelical tradition. They are churches that preserve the lay dominance of that era and often allow women great freedom of expression and service. All of these groups are carful to uphold the unique nature of the church under God's spirit.

And finally a third type of response to over "professionalization" has been the renewed interest in small group life within the mainline churches. This renewal has taken many forms, sometimes sparked by professionals themselves. The thrust here is to recapture some of the past pattern of vital lay involvement with issues in the churches. Groups gather for Bible study, to discuss some book or article, or to learn about each other. In each case, however, the laity take initiative and share leadership. Lay retreats, seminars, prayer groups, underground churches and house churches all blur the lines between specialist and client. When that happens the church is reconstituted as the body of Christ made up of many members, each valued and important. The lay strength of American denominationalism is reaffirmed in these developments.

The contemporary problem is that ministry is becoming an increasingly professionalized vocation. The pressure for theological education and training for ministry is increasing, even among new groups formed in reaction to professionalism. These general social pressures for education and specialization are operating with great power. A liberal seminary, such as CTS, is receiving applications from persons in denominational traditions that have been satisfied with Bible college degrees in the past.

From the standpoint of theological education this is good. We believe that an educated ministry is a social benefit, or we would not be here. We exist to enrich the life of the churches.

At the same time, economic changes are forcing theological education to examine its commitment to specialization and narrow professionalism. In the last decade the increased costs of specialized ministries have radically reduced opportunities for professional ministry outside of the local parish. We can no longer afford ministerial specialists. Today the call is for generalists who can preach, teach, counsel, organize, etc., or even hold down a secular job to pay the bills. In one sense we need more skilled professionals able to balance competing claims for time and talent. In another sense we need a non-professional, or a new professional who can enable and support laity in the life of the church, rather than do it all him/herself as a sort of "super minister." Economic circumstances and social pressures are forcing American denominations to reclaim the power of the laity so characteristic of our heritage.

This development presents particular problems and opportunities to women. Egalitarian education has opened the doors to theological study for hundreds of women. It is no secret that seminary enrollments are increasingly showing high percentages of women students. Whether these women are coming to seminary out of their frustration with women's work in country club churches, or out of their new-found freedom in evangelical groups, or out of their personal experience in some lay seminar, retreat or house church — these women **are** in seminary. Women have been relegated to lay status for so long that it feels good to us to say, "I want to be ordained," "I want to be a professional," "I want to do ministry as well as, or better than the men — indeed, I **will**!"

But there is a hidden problem here. In some instances these eager-to-be professionals are buying into a definition of ministry which is counterproductive. As women struggle to become assertive, self-confident equals in professional ministry, they perpetuate some of the very problems they went into ministry to solve. I understand this problem. My very presence on an otherwise all male theological faculty partakes of that dilemma.

It is important for me and for all women in ministry to recognize our lay heritage. American denominationalism was built upon the strength of the laity, particularly women. As women in contemporary churches, we need to consider the nature of ministry and the choices before us. We can join the professional club and seek to outdo our male colleagues in professional competence. In some ways we need to do this in order to prove to ourselves and everyone that we can. But, in view of the needs and problems of ministry in the 1970s, women have a unique calling.

I believe that effective ministry for the future will affirm the shared responsibility of the people of God. In America this means a reclamation of our strong history of lay leadership, particularly the work of women. It may be that the contemporary feminist movement in the churches can be a channel for the rediscovery of this tradition. Women in ministry creating a collaborative enabling style of professional life are in a unique position to use professional skills for lay empowerment. This is particularly appropriate because women have historically been the lay energy of the churches in America.

Where two or three are gathered together, Christians have recognized the church. In the American tradition our piety and practicality have caused us to develop a denominationalism affirming pluralism. This denominationalism has in turn been characterized by strong lay participation, particularly that of women. In the twentieth century, however, the churches have tended to become professionalized and the laity reduced to subservience. It is important, therefore, as we strive to reclaim lay life in the churches, that the special opportunities open to women be proclaimed. Women have a calling to be professional and lay leaders. Women have a history that points toward an enabling collaborative style of ministry. Women have something unique to offer the churches of today and tomorrow.

NOTES:

The section of this paper devoted to an exposition of "denominationalism" is indebted to the work of Winthrop Hudson. See particularly "Denominationalism as a Basis for Ecumenicity," *Church History*, XXIV (1955), pp. 37-47 and *American Protestantism* (Chicago: University of Chicago, 1961), pp. 33-48. A more contemporary analysis of this tradition is found in Andrew M. Greeley, *The Denominational Society: A Sociological Approach to Religion in America* (Glenview, Ill.: Scott, Foresman, 1972).

Writings on the lay tradition in American religion are difficult to locate. I am indebted to a chapter by Howard Grimes, "The United States, 1800-1962" in Stephen Charles Neill and Hans-Ruedi Weber (eds.), *The Layman in Christian History* (Philadelphia: Westminster, 1963), pp. 240-260.

Material which focuses upon the general contributions of lay women in American history can be found in Elsie Thomas Culver, *Women in the World of Religion* (Garden City, N.J.: Doubleday, 1967) and Georgia Harkness, *Women in Church and Society* (Nashville and New York: Abingdon, 1972).

Two more specialized books on women in the antislavery movement and world mission work are: Alma Lutz, *Crusade for Freedom* (Boston: Beacon, 1968) and R. Pierce Beaver, *All Loves Excelling* (Grand Rapids, Mich.: Eerdmans, 1968).

Many of the above resources are out of print. There is one general volume on women in American life that is currently available in a paper-bound edition. Although it is not descriptive of the church, it offers a good overview. Emily Hahn, *Once Upon a Pedestal* (New York: Mentor, 1974). The Harkness book is also available in paperback.

LIFESTYLE AS A RELIGIOUS AND ETHICAL ISSUE IN AMERICAN THOUGHT

By PERRY LeFEVRE

In their two hundred years, the American people have lived through a revolution, a civil war, economic depressions, two great foreign wars, the loss of confidence in our own national government in the Watergate affair. Crises of a different kind and of a worldwide character have come into our awareness within the last generation — the energy crisis, the ecological crisis, the population crisis, the crisis of world hunger. These matters have been analyzed and exposed in a series of doomsday reports produced by both individuals and groups of concerned intellectuals (e.g., Heilbroner's *The Human Prospect,* the Club of Rome reports, etc.).[1] The situation which these reports reflect has brought about fundamental questioning of both individual and cultural lifestyles. Those who have been most deeply concerned with the critical issues facing all of us have come to see that the varied crises are in fact not primarily technological in character but are individually and collectively crises of meaning. The root problems are ethical and religious. The issues are value issues; what needs reexamination are the values for which our culture and each of us as individuals live.

Out of this crisis of meaning and the call to reexamine our basic values there has been a growing movement toward the simplification of lifestyle. This movement is itself a critique of the prodigal son lifestyle of culture and individual and a positive searching for a more meaningful and creative life for persons and society.

In this bicentennial year it has seemed to me worthwhile to reexamine this issue of lifestyle in light of the American past and to do this by focusing directly on some of the most forceful critiques of individual and societal values in the views of those who called men and women to a simpler mode of life. I am interested in discovering not only the nature and depth of the criticism but also in uncovering the basic ethical and religious convictions which underlie such criticism. Such an effort may feed our own thinking with respect to our contemporary questions.

Apart from the monastic movements, the left wing of the Reformation produced the most consistent and persistent call for the simplification of lifestyle in Western Christendom.[2] The classic American statement of this point of view is that of John Woolman in his *Journal* and in his essay *A Plea for the Poor.* Woolman was an eighteenth century Quaker tailer who was one of the most sensitive ethical spirits this nation has produced. He not only developed an ethic and theology for the simple life; he practiced it.

Woolman writes that until 1756 he engaged himself both in the sale of retail goods and in the tailoring business, but that he became uneasy as he found that business became too cumbersome. "I felt a stop in my mind," he writes. He came to see the need for a simpler way of life. He therefore lessened his outward business and learned to be content with "a plain way of living."[3]

What lay behind Woolman's own adoption of the plain way of life was not only a sensitive spirit but a clarity of ethical and religious analysis which has seldom been equaled in American religious thought concerning lifestyle.

The basic presupposition of Woolman's view is religious or theological: "Truth did not require me to engage in much cumbrous affairs."[4] "Truth" here does not mean "truths", but rather "ultimate spiritual reality" — divinity, God as known in Jesus Christ. What underlies this conviction is Woolman's sense of proportion, or perhaps better, his sense of importance. God had more important things for Woolman and for all human beings to do than "getting and spending." Simple living frees the human spirit for the pursuit of a greater good for one's fellow human beings and for oneself. "To labor for an establishment in divine love where the mind is disentangled from the power of darkness is the great business of man's life."[5] A simple life style enables the service of divine love in the world and at the same time, where people are "content with a plain way of life . . . there is more true peace and calmness of mind than those have had who aspiring to greatness and outward show, have grasped hard for an income to support themselves in it."[6]

Such is the positive thrust of Woolman's teaching on the simple life. There is, however, a major negative critique of the existing cultural and individual lifestyles which surrounded him. His critique has a prophetic character as he points to the immediate and long range implications of the pursuit of wealth and luxury for both individuals and society.

The striving for luxurious living makes for an anxious, selfish and covetous spirit. It leads to people working harder than they ought or would need to. A plain way of life would make it possible for work to be "more agreeable," "without the oppression of always striving."[7] Woolman held that the divine wisdom did not intend that human beings should become oppressed with striving and overburdened with labor.

Bad as the abandonment of the simple life was for the individual, its societal implications were foreboding. Speaking of the use of slaves to strive for wealth, Woolman wrote: "And here luxury and covetousness, with the numerous oppressions and other evils attending them, appeared very affecting to me, and I felt in that which is immutable that the seeds of great calamity and desolation are sown and growing fast on this continent."[8]

Though Woolman was one of America's most forceful and sensitive critics of slavery, it was not only the oppression of fellow human beings which offended his moral sense. Oxen and horses were likewise oppressed and for the same pursuit of gain.

> Oxen and horses are often seen at work when, through heat and too much labor, their eyes and the emotion of their bodies manifest that they are oppressed. Their loads in wagons are frequently so heavy that when weary with hauling it far, their drivers find occasion in going up hills or through mire to raise their spirits by whipping to get forward.[9]

Such action is "contrary to the gracious design of him who is the true owner of the earth; nor can any possessions, either acquired or derived from ancestors justify such conduct."[10]

The collecting of wealth, covering the body with "fine-wrought apparel," having magnificient furnishings "operates against universal love and tends to feed the self . . ."[11] This "feeding of the self" not only leads one to oppress others but it leads to a whole way of life contrary to the humility and plainness modeled by Jesus. Woolman sees the spirit which loves riches and luxury as lying behind a self-protective lifestyle which leads to war, to military preparedness, to the slave trade, and to all manner of human degradations. The desire to attain wealth is like a first link in a chain. "This desire being cherished moves to action, and riches thus gotten please self, and while self hath a life in them it desires to have them defended."

> If we consider the havoc that is made in this age, and how numbers of people are hurried on, striving to collect treasures to please that mind which wanders from perfect resignedness, and in that wisdom which is foolishness with God are perverting the true use of things, labouring as in the fire, contending with one another even unto blood, and exerting their power to support ways of living foreign to the life of one wholly crucified to the world; if we consider what great numbers of people are employed in different kingdoms in preparing the materials of war, and the labour and toil of armies set apart for protecting their respective territories from the incursions of others, and the extensive miseries which attend their engage-

ments; while many of those who till the lands and are employed in other useful things—in supporting themselves, supporting those employed in military affairs, and some who own the soil—have great hardships to encounter through too much labour; while others in several kingdoms are busied in fetching men to help labour from distant parts of the world, to spend the remainder of their lives in the uncomfortable condition of slaves, and that self is at the bottom of these proceedings—amidst all this confusion, and these scenes of sorrow and distress, can we remember the Prince of Peace, re- member that we are his disciples, and remember that example of humility and plainness which he set for us, without feeling an ear- nest desire to be disentangled from everything connected with sel- fish customs in food, in raiment, in houses, and all things else; that being of Christ's family and walking as he walked, we may stand in that uprightness wherein man was first made, and have no fellowship with those invention which men in the fallen wisdom have sought out."[12]

Were Americans to adopt simple plain lifestyles they would not only have time to give to really important concerns, but says Woolman, in a paragraph which might be part of a contemporary argument for the sup- port of teachers and schools, they would then have resources for the significant things which need doing:

Were we thoroughly weaned from the love of wealth and fully brought out of all superfluities in living, employments about vani- ties being finished and labour wanted only for things consistent with a humble, self-denying life, there would on a reasonable estimate be so much to spare on the education of our children that a plain, humble man with a family like himself might be furnished with a living for teaching and overseeing so small a number of children that he might properly and seasonably administer to each individual, and gently lead them on as the Gospel Spirit opened the way, with- out giving countenance to pride or evil emulation amongst them.[13]

HENRY THOREAU

From the eighteenth century to the nineteenth, from Quaker saint to transcendentalist poet and naturalist is quite a leap, but Henry Thoreau was an equally articulate critic of the individual and cultural lifestyles of his day and an equally powerful advocate of the simple life. His book, *Walden*, stands as one of the great American documents for any counter- culture.

Like Woolman, Thoreau is moved by his own sense of importance and value. He sees his fellow human beings spending their lives on what ap- pear to him to be trivia. We "live meanly like ants." "Our life is frittered away by detail."[14] As a result the quality of life is missed. "Most men . . . are so occupied with the factitious cares and superflously coarse la- bors of life that its finer fruits cannot be plucked by them."[15] They are crushed and smothered under the load of things. They creep down the road of life. They have mean and sneaking lives, lives of "quiet desperation." Incessant anxiety and strain mark human existence. Why is this so? It is, says Thoreau, because they "are employed, as it says in the old book, laying up treasures which moth and rust will corrupt and thieves break through and steal. It is a fool's life, as they will find when they get to the end of it, if not before."[16] Slavery is not limited to the South says Thoreau; "many are their own slave drivers" . . . as if you could kill time without injuring eternity."[17]

We should, says Thoreau, consider what is actually necessary for life. Most luxuries and many of what we regard as comforts of life are not only not necessary, but are positive hindrances to the elevation of mankind. "Simplicity, simplicity, simplicity," he writes. "Simplify, Simplify." "Instead of three meals a day, if it be necessary, eat but one; instead of a hundred dishes, five; and reduce other things in proportion."[18] The whole nation "lives too fast."

> Men think that it is essential that the Nation have commerce, and export ice, and talk through a telegraph, and ride thirty miles an hour, without a doubt whether they do or not; but whether we should live like baboons or like men, is a little uncertain.[19]

It is not the pace or intensity of life in itself which is questionable. Rather, it is that we miss what is really important. We live on the surface of life. Our "vision does not penetrate" below that surface. "We think that that which **is** which **appears** to be." Truth and eternity appear to be far off, but that is not the case, says Thoreau. "God himself culminates in the present moment, and will never be more divine in the lapse of all the ages."[20]

Thoreau believes that if one simplifies one's life one will undergo a reversal of one's perception and understanding. "In proportion as he simplifies his life, the law of the universe will appear less complex, and solitude will not be solitude, nor poverty poverty, nor weakness weakness." "Why should we be in such desperate haste to succeed in such desperate enterprises," asks Thoreau? "If a man does not keep pace with his companions, perhaps it is because he hears a different drummer. Let him step to the music he hears, however measured or far away."[21]

THORSTEIN VEBLEN

Thorstein Veblen marched to a different drummer, and though he was neither Quaker saint nor transcendentalist mystic, he was an articulate analyst of the cultural lifestyle of his own time. Some may think it strange to find Veblen treated in a study of the ethical and religious perspectives on lifestyle. Certainly he was a sharp critic of religious faith and institutions, and at least in the works we have under discussion he disowns moral concern. His *Theory of the Leisure Class* purports to be purely "scientific." Words which would for most of us be value terms are used says Veblen descriptively and without moral judgment. It is true that Veblen wants to be taken for a sceintist and that on one side he is a methodological behaviorist. But, as David Seckler puts it, there are "two Veblens,"[22] a humanistic Veblen as well as a scientific one, and the loaded language, the satire and invective are clearly not value neutral whatever Veblen claims on the face of it.

Veblen's theory of the cultural lifestyle centers around such terms as "conspicuous consumption," "conspicuous leisure", "ostentatious waste."

> The keystone of contemporary culture, is simple ostentatious waste — of money, time, resources, and effort. Our notions of the true, the good, the beautiful are modelled by the imperative of conspicuous waste, and accordingly, since these notions are what makes life worth living, our lives are energetically devoted to that cause.[23]

Why this should be so is what *The Theory of the Leisure Class* is about. So long as there was no surplus beyond what was actually needed for life, wasteful consumption was hardly possible. With a surplus, emulation entered in. Invidious distinctions were drawn. Prestige came from wealth and from the leisure and conspicuous consumption that symbolized wealth to others. The utility of conspicuous leisure and consumption for reputability "lies in the element of waste that is common to both . . . In order to be reputable it must be wasteful."[24]

Like Thoreau and Woolman, Veblen sees a culture in which accumulation and use go far beyond necessity, but instead of seeing that work and striving exceed necessity, Veblen points to the invidious use of leisure and consumption as symbols of wealth and power. They are the basis for establishing both regard and self-regard through comparison with others. If Veblen were a theologian, we might say that he came much closer to a doctrine of original sin both in its individual and social aspects than did Woolman and Thoreau. "Emulation," "invidious distinction," and "exploit" channel the basic instincts of "workmanship," "idle curiosity," and "parental bent" into what Veblen believes must ultimately be self-destructive directions. His Darwinianism suggests that the sheer precariousness of human existence will make "wastemanship" self-destructing. And he may be right. "Waste" may be useful or functional from the point of view of the consumer and yet ultimately non-functional for human life as a whole, and hence in the long run self-defeating.

Veblen also goes beyond Thoreau and Woolman in his emphasis on the cultural dimensions of lifestyle, particularly in seeing the power of cultural influences on individuals and groups. The real carriers of conspicuous leisure and conspicuous consumption as lifestyles are class habits, standards, and tastes. Individuals do not necessarily decide self-consciously for this way of life. More often individuals simply absorb certain attitudes, expectations, behaviors from their own culture or subculture.

The third distinctive contribution of Veblen is his understanding that the principles of emulation and invidious comparison may well be insatiable. He writes:

> In a general way the need for expenditure grows as fast as the means of satisfying it, and, in the long run, a larger expenditure comes no nearer to satisfying the desire than a smaller one . . . No advance in the average well-being of the community can end the struggle or lessen the strain.[25]

It is this fact which is at the root of the dissatisfactions with capitalism, and it is this which stands behind the thrust to what some think might be socialist equality. No matter how much improvement there is in the economic well-being, the principle of emulation infects human and social relations. Status, not actual well-being, is what moves the economic and social machine. The consumers "can be relied on to purchase as much as can conceivably be made."[26]

Each generation, each historical period seems to produce its own critics — those who are sensitive enough to transcend the culturally dominant values of a given time and place. We have singled out an eighteenth century Quaker as critic of the world of colonial America with its agricultural and slave economy, a nineteenth century individualist protesting the loss of eternity in the drivenness and busy-ness of a society dominated by trade and commerce, an early twentieth century secular prophet, whose *Theory of the Leisure Class* (1899), while its theoretical sweep included the whole of human history, reflected the exploitative industrial society of an America reaching affluence built upon waste.

LEWIS MUMFORD

With the figure of Lewis Mumford we come to our own day and to one whose historical purview is as large as any of the others. And once again the basic criticism of individual and cultural lifestyle is grounded in the problematic of meaning and value. Every civilization, says Mumford, comes to face its own crisis of meaning. It becomes so complex, so overorganized, so immersed in the multiplication of superfluous wants, so routinized and fossilized that "the preparatory acts deplete the appropriate consummations."[27] In such an existence

> people eat for the sake of supporting meat packers' organizations and dairymen's associations, they guard their health carefully for the sake of creating dividends for their life insurance corporations, they earn their daily living for the sake of paying dues, taxes, mortgages, installments on their car or their television sets, or fulfilling their quota in a Five Year Plan: in short, they satisfy the essential needs of life for extraneous reasons.

Such a society "ties itself into knots by its inability to put first things first."[28]

Since no community can permit itself to be stalled for long there will come a time of forced choice. Either Burckhardt's "Terrible Simplifiers" will take over — "What the virtuous will not do in a reasonable and constructive way, the criminal and barbarian take upon themselves to do, negatively and irrationally, for the sheer pleasure of destruction." — Or the benign simplifiers will, with art and reason, give back authority to the human person:

> Life belongs to the free-living and mobile creatures, not to the encrusted ones; and to restore the initiative to life and to participate in its renewal, we must counterbalance every fresh complexity, every mechanical refinement, every increase in quantitative goods or quantitative knowledge, every advance in manipulative technique, every threat of superabundance or surfeit, with stricter habits of evaluation, rejection, choice

We must consciously resist

> every kind of automatism: buy nothing merely because it is advertised, use no invention merely because it has been put on the market, follow no practice merely because it is fashionable. We must approach every part of our lives with the spirit in which Thoreau undertook his housekeeping at Walden Pond: be ready, like him, even to throw out a simple stone, if it proves too much trouble to dust.[29]

There is no domain, says Mumford, where methods of simplification must not be introduced. The only true salvation is to increase our selectivity. The whole routine of life comes under this dictum:

> never to use mechanical power when human muscles can conveniently do the work, never to use a motor car where one might easily walk, never to acquire information or knowledge except for the satisfaction of some immediate or prospective wants.[30]

Mumford points out that the complusive use of tobacco and alcohol, the waste involved in following fashion as indicative of the "depth of our perversion of life-needs" in a time when fellow human beings are starving.[31] Simplicity does not mean repudiation of the machine. It means only that we should not be victimized by machines:

> Wherever the machine is intelligently adapted to human needs, it has the effect of simplifying the routine of life and releasing the human agent from slavish mechanical tasks. It is only when the person abdicates that mechanization presents a threat.

Simplicity for Mumford is not its own goal. The purpose is to use simplicity to promote spontaneity and freedom, "so that we may do justice to life's new occasions and singular moments . . . This reduction to essentials is the main art of life."[32]

The cultural critique which Mumford produced in his *The Conduct of Life* (1951) and the simplification of life which he called for were directed at the dehumanization of contemporary American urban and industrial civilization. He called for renewal based on the primacy of the person over the machine. An even more sober Mumford writes today in his eighties of a "vision of a world different from that which comforts, or, at best, only slightly discomforts many of my contemporaries."[33]

He writes:

> It seems to me that, on the basis of rational calculations, derived from what must admittedly be incomplete evidence, if the forces that now dominate us continue on their present path they must lead to collapse of the whole historical fabric, not just this or that great nation or empire . . .

> To flinch now from facing these realities and evaluating them is to me an act of intellectual cowardice. But because I have dared to face and evaluate them I have often been dismissed as a 'prophet of doom.' This is no more intelligent than to say to a physician who diagnoses a possible fatal disease and applies his skill to curing it that he is a willing ally of the undertaker.

> On the contrary, every fibre of my being revolts against the fate that threatens our civilization, and revolts almost equally against those supine minds that accept it as inevitable, or, even, worse, seek treasonably to justify its inevitability.[34]

The contemporary global crises of poverty, overpopulation, ecological disaster, and energy exhaustion are the realities which threaten the collapse of the whole historical fabric of civilization. More and more I think we are coming to realize that it is only in a secondary sense that these crises are technological in character. In this light, there is no "technological fix" which will save us. The real crisis is religious and ethical. It is a crisis in meaning and value.

I have lately come to feel that Tolstoy's story "The Death of Ivan Illich" is a parable for our culture. Suddenly the question of what we have been living for and what is the real good of life is raised for us by the prospect of cultural death. In the midst of this crisis of meaning and value some individuals and groups have withdrawn from full cultural participation. Others, chiefly of the college age, launched a major countercultural movement during the period of the Vietnam war. How much power or residual impact these persons have for cultural change is uncertain.

Other individuals and groups concerned with special aspects of the contemporary crisis—energy, poverty, population, ecology, work on their own "thing" which is indeed everyone's thing if everyone only knew it. Certainly their efforts lead to changes in individual lifestyle and to the degree that the general consciousness of the society is raised may bring about some change in the cultural lifestyle. It is doubtful, however, how much lasting impact there is. The energy crisis raises consciousness and we have a momentary turn to small cars and other conservation efforts, but only a few months pass, the crisis seems over, and the turn is back to large cars once again. This may be symbolic of the depth of our problem of meaning.

A few, reaching out from religious roots, have called for and pledged themselves to the development of simple lifestyles. Symbolic of this are the Simple Living Program of the American Friends Service Committee of San Francisco and the issue of the Shakertown Pledge drawn up by staff members of religious retreat centers in 1974. The Shakertown Pledge is itself a kind of summary of both the crisis of meaning and value and a purposive response to it that reaches below the level of technological solutions to individual and cultural lifestyle.

THE SHAKERTOWN PLEDGE

Recognizing that the earth and the fullness thereof is a gift from God, and that we are called to cherish, nurture, and provide loving stewardship for the earth's resources,

And recognizing that life itself is a gift, and a call to responsibility, joy, and celebration,

I make the following declarations:

1. I declare myself to be a world citizen. (Or, I recognize that I am a world citizen, and that all the peoples of the earth are my neighbors.)

2. I commit myself to lead an ecologically sound life.

3. I commit myself to occupational responsibility. I will seek to avoid the creation of products which work others harm.

4. I commit myself to personal renewal through meditation, prayer, and reflection.

5. I affirm the gift that is my body, and pledge that I will attend to its proper nourishment and physical fitness.

6. I pledge myself to examine continually my relations with others, and to attempt to relate honestly, morally, and lovingly to those around me.

7. I commit myself to responsible participation in a community of faith.

8. I commit myself to leading a life of creative simplicity, and to sharing my personal wealth with the world's poor.

9. I pledge myself to join with others in the reshaping of institutions in order to bring about a more just global society in which each person has full access to the needed resources for their physical, emotional, intellectual, and spiritual growth.

None of us can know how great the responsive power and the resilience of the culture are to this crisis of meaning and value. Perhaps as Barbara Ward has suggested in the February 1976 issue of **Pro Veritate,** the situation is one in which the great ethical traditions of mankind, and especially that of the Christian tradition, can be "listened to with entirely new attention." She points to the moral imperatives found in these traditions — "the need to share, to love, to respect, to use material things with contraint, not to be greedy, not to be rapacious, not to make wealth at all costs the end of life."

Today, she says, this is not just preacher talk, prophet talk, saint talk. We have reached the point where if we "do not practice the traditional virtues we are probably not going to survive."

> So the prophets, the mystics, and the saints whom we have dismissed as highly metaphysical but not particularly relevant turn out to be the genuine realists, the men and women most fitted to survive. The vows taken by religious bodies, of poverty, obedience and loving restraint, for this is one of the meanings of chastity, are symbols of the kind of vow whole societies have to consider . . . The realism proposed by the gospels is the realism of survival. The realism of those who would tell us that we can go on wastefully and selfishly as we do now, is the realism of death.

"If," she concludes, "our practice is evidence of a new life in us, it will be attended to in quite a new way. Because of this, the responsibility is all the greater but so also are the reasons for happiness and hope."[35]

NOTES:

1. Robert L. Heilbroner, *An Inquiry into the Human Prospect*, Norton, 1974. Donella H. Meadows et al, *The Limits to Growth*, Universe Books, 1972.
2. For example in the 20th century a significant number of essays and "tracts for the times": Richard B. Gregg, *The Value of Voluntary Simplicity*, Pendle Hill Phamphlet No. 3, 1936; Thomas R. Kelly, *A Testament of Devotion*, Harper, 1941; Mildred B. Young, *Another Will Gird Your*, Pendle Hill Pamphlet No. 109, 1960; *A Standard of Living*, Pendle Hill Pamphlet No. 12, 1941; *What Doth the Lord Require of Thee*, Pendle Hill Pamphlet No. 145, 1966; Arthur G. Gish, *Beyond the Rat Race*, Herald Press, 1973; Vernard Eller, *The Simple Life*, Eerdmanns, 1973.
3. *The Journal and Major Essays of John Woolman*, Edited by Phillips P. Moulton, Oxford, 1971, p. 53.
4. *Ibid.*
5. *Ibid.*, p. 250.
6. *Ibid.*, p. 114-15.
7. *Ibid.*, p. 118-19.
8. *Ibid.*, p. 129.
9. *Ibid.*, p. 238.
10. *Ibid.*, p. 239.
11. *Ibid.*, p. 250.
12. *Ibid.*, p. 253.

13. *Ibid.,* p. 264.
14. Henry D. Thoreau, *Walden,* Peter Pauper Press, n.d., p. 82.
15. *Ibid.,* p. 10.
16. *Ibid.,* p. 9.
17. *Ibid.,* p. 11.
18. *Ibid.,* p. 82.
19. *Ibid.*
20. *Ibid.,* pp. 86-87.
21. *Ibid.,* p. 287.
22. David Seckler, *Thorstein Veblen and the Institutionalists,* Colorado Associated University Press, 1975, p. 8.
23. *Ibid.,* p. 42.
24. Thorstein Veblen, *The Theory of the Leisure Class,* The Modern Library, 1934, p. 85 and p. 96.
25. Quoted by Seckler, *op. cit.,* p. 40 from Veblen "Some Neglected Points in the Theory of Socialism" (1891).
26. Seckler, *op. cit.,* p. 45.
27. Lewis Mumford, *The Conduct of Life,* Harcourt Brace, 1951, p. 269.
28. *Ibid.,* p. 268.
29. *Ibid.,* p. 270.
30. *Ibid.,* p. 271.
31. *Ibid.,* p. 272.
32. *Ibid.,* p. 273.
33. Lewis Mumford, *Findings and Keepings,* Harcourt Brace, 1975, p. 380.
34. *Ibid.,* p. 382.
35. *Op. cit.,* p. 12.

THE BIBLE AS A WEAPON IN EVANGELICAL-LIBERAL WARFARE[1]

By ROBIN SCROGGS

In the flaming sixties, American liberal religious leaders were turned largely toward secular culture. This was in part because of their sense of social responsibility. But in large part too it was determined by their awareness that our age was a post-Christian age, that Christianity was now a minority cult in a sea of secularism, that the most desperately needed evangelism was somehow to speak religiously and yet convincingly to the cultured despisers. With-it theologians created novel contents and structures for their theologies and a whole pop-culture of theological tracts emerged. A death-of-God theologian, writing as late as 1971, argued that the only kind of Christianity which could possibly have any apologetic appeal to the world at large was one in which belief in God was not part of the package.[2]

The biblical heritage was relegated by many to the archaic and irrelevant past. When I joined the CTS faculty in 1969, it quickly became obvious to me that I would have to fight hard even to get seminary students to look seriously at the Bible. Only that which is evolving into the future needs to claim one's serious attention.

If anyone had, in those disturbing and yet challenging days, whispered in my ear, "What do you think of the Scopes trial?", it would have taken me awhile to recover **that** time and space and **that** memory of a bitter, sibling quarrel. Once I had, I would have smiled and realized that the memory was of a bad dream — and somebody else's bad dream at that. I was persuaded that the issue of biblical literalism was long dead and would never emerge again. Of course I knew there were still groups loosely, and in part inaccurately, called 'fundamentalists'; but I relegated them to the minority and weak fringes of the church.

My vision, however, was myopic; for my attention was then so focused on the challenge of secularism that I never thought to look over my shoulder to see another force just then gathering energy and marshalling forces to reenter the battle for the hearts of the American people. Religious conservatism, like a sleeping giant suddenly awakened, has wrestled its way back into the ring. It is a formidable opponent.

But while it caught the liberal off guard, the current expansion of the conservative church is no mutation. The evangelical (better so named than 'fundamentalist') churches are just today beginning to reap the harvest of a long but careful building of institutions and programs. The conservative denominations are growing, some more rapidly than others — but at any rate not losing members as are the mainline establishment churches. Educational institutions of significance have been created by the evangelicals to meet the needs of the evangelicals. The conservative seminaries are, it would seem, growing at a faster rate than are those of the mainline. A new breed of conservative scholars has emerged, with degrees from reputable institutions and with the requisite skills and sophistication to argue for the evangelical cause in a non-simplistic manner, (e.g., Henry). Fuller Theological Seminary is today the center — and a strong one at that — for the thinking evangelical.

What those of us in the liberal tradition must realize is that this time there is going to be no apparently easy victory like that symbolized by the Scopes trial, which so seriously disorganized and routed the fundamentalist forces in the late twenties. The evangelical is here to stay; our first task is to recognize this and, in so far as is possible, greet him like the brother he actually is. Our second task is to bring ourselves up to date on what has been happening in our recent past, so that we understand where the evangelical comes from and what he understands the truth to be. We must recover the past in order to understand our present. Thus my purpose in this paper is to trace as simply as possible the very complex movements within American religious history of the nineteenth and twentieth century that have caused the liberal-conservative split to emerge. Only in this way can we have the perspective to understand and hopefully, to influence the present.

One thing is clear. The Bible has from the beginning been the focus of the argument and thus will be the focus of this paper. But here two things need to be kept in mind. 1) **Both** sides have claimed the Bible for themselves. Each side has used the Bible as its key weapon. Obviously very different understandings of what Scripture means are at stake. 2) Just this fact suggests that much is going on that is **purely external to the Bible.** What factors caused the literalist to claim his own interpretation of the Bible as truth (and therefore not really an interpretation at all)? The same question can be put to the liberal. These external factors are diverse and diffuse; they include sociological, psychological, and philosophical dimensions. In this paper it is impossible to deal with this problem, but I cannot overstate the importance of always being aware that **any** statement of the meaning of the Bible **is** an interpretation and that this interpretation does not stem from the Bible itself but is based on some claim which is antecedent, historically and logically, to the interpretation itself.

THE BACKGROUND OF THE LIBERAL-EVANGELICAL CONTROVERSY

The so-called fundamentalist/modernist controversy came into the open no earlier than the last quarter of the nineteenth century, but the battle was brewing at least from the beginning of that century. Classically the church had held varied and sophisticated views of the proper interpretation of Scripture, and an explicit view of literal, verbal inspiration was never dominant. The notions of self-conscious American literalists would have seemed to the trained Medieval interpreter a peculiar and even bizarre foreshortening of the richness of the hermeneutical tradition of the church. For example, Luther, separating revelation from the words of Scripture, could never have agreed with the American literalists. The literalists have claimed Calvin as support, but even here the evidence does not seem to support the claim.[3] Of course all would have concurred that the Bible was inspired, breathed into by the Spirit of God; but it is precisely over what inspiration means that the views diverged.

However the causes may be explained, early nineteenth century American evangelicals, seeking a simple and secure basis for faith, chose to stand on a Bible which they claimed had been **in each word** inspired by God. Every word and phrase was exactly what God wished to say to His people. Just **how** this happened was in most instances wisely rejected as a discussible issue; the results, not the means, of inspiration was all they cared to claim.

Consonant with this emphasis on **verbal** inspiration was a similar emphasis upon **historical** literalism. The possibility that God **intended** to speak poetically or metaphorically, that is, non-literally, was mostly rejected. Thus Genesis one describes what actually happened in creation. This view has special importance for the prophetic literature. The prophets were seen as predicting historical happenings future to them; these events must have already been fulfilled or are yet to be fulfilled. There were many disputes about **when** the events in the Book of Revelation were to take place; but **that** they were to happen as the author describes them was common agreement.

The seriousness of the program of these evangelicals is seen in their absolute refusal to compromise on the issue. From their perspective, it was an either/or. One chink in the armour brings down the whole fortress. Thus if the Bible is proved 'wrong' at any point, (which they equated with being historically inaccurate in a literal way), it somehow becomes worthless. As one writer put it, "To be God's book, it must be His in matter and in words, in substance and in form" (Sandeen, p. 111). Thus it is clear from the beginning that an extreme position has been adopted such that **any** other view not only cannot be absorbed but must be seen as an enemy. This extremity of position both explains and is symptomatic of the complete rigidity, not to say brittleness, of nineteenth and early twentieth century literalism.

One might be tempted to conclude that such views could be explained by the American frontier spirit, of uneducated people deifying their sense of common sense, but this is not the case. Some literalists were, of course, on the frontier and were largely self-educated. Yet their views do not seem to have differed from the professors who taught in that bastion of intellectual Presbyterianism, Princeton Seminary (Sandeen, pp. 103-31). Throughout the century this institution was guided and controlled by intellectuals and scholars who mounted exactly the same program of complete verbal inspiration. Indeed, the earlier statements from the Seminary do not seem to have taken into account what the scholars themselves doubtlessly knew, that scribal errors abound in the ancient manuscripts, that decision as to the correct reading is delicate, and that translations of the Hebrew and Greek into modern languages always involve human judgment. The implication of the Princeton position was that the Bible in its present form, and perhaps that extends to the translations, is the inspired Word. If so, God speaks with a forked tongue.

It is only later in the century that the Princeton professors, apparently under pressure from historical criticism, distinguished between the verbal inspiration of the **original autographs** and the scribal transmissions, which they acknowledged were not inspired as were the now lost original manuscripts. They were quick to point out a true fact, that this concession did not seriously undermine the **content** of Scripture, since for all the myriads of textual variants very little that is central to the biblical message is called into question by such variants. But it certainly is a serious retreat from the basic **theory**, at least to the extent that the theory is designed to give people complete confidence that the present Scripture is the direct, unmediated revelation from God.

One popular expression of nineteenth century American evangelicalism was millennialism. The millennialist lives in the faith that the cataclysmic events associated by biblical apocalyptic with the end-times and the reign in the messianic kingdom of the Book of Revelation are events which are expected to happen soon. It was also a hope of participating in that 1000-year reign of bliss. As one scholar describes it, "America in the early nineteenth century was drunk on the millennium" (Sandeen, p. 42). It was one way people had of expressing their optimistic or pessimistic views about history. It became a convenient language for Americans, steeped in the Bible, to interpret the contemporary historical scene. If one were an optimist about America and its manifest destiny, he became a **post-millennialist**. That is, he believed that human history would know a prolonged period of peaceful perfection **before** Christ returned to the earth. If one were a pessimist — and this view eventually won in this country, in large part due to Calvinist views on the depravity of humanity and **despite** the emerging sense of manifest destiny — one became a **pre-millennialist.** That is, he did not anticipate a period of historical perfection. History would, in fact, get continually worse; and Christ would appear **before** the millennium. Only then could any perfection be imagined. This was a view of the sovereignty of the graceful God over against the depravity of humanity.

It would be interesting to speculate how this relates to the appropriation of Darwinian evolutionary theories by liberal theologians. The doctrine of Christian progressivism is perhaps the liberal correlate to the evangelical post-millennialism. If so, the victory of pre-millennialism within evangelicalism is set off against the growing optimism within liberalism. Evangelicals retained the reformed pessimism about human nature; liberals moved to a novel (and thus from the perspective of the evangelicals, heretical) view of humanity as perfectible and as progressing toward that perfection.

For our purposes it is crucial to note that millennialist views were made possible by a literalist interpretation of Scripture but can hardly be said to be necessitated by it. (One can be a literalist without affirming the millennialist position.) This seems to me a classic example of how the Bible can become the vehicle to express deep-rooted desires and fears. Biblical language was such a part of the American experience that it would have been difficult to choose another vehicle. From today's vantage, it is easy to say that neither millennialism nor Darwinian progressivism has adequate perspectives from which to interpret Scripture. Nineteenth century theologians could not see it that way.

One final point. I have avoided in this paper the most popular title for the Christian literalist, namely 'fundamentalist'. I have done so because 'fundamentalism' properly should be limited to describe believers who lifted up certain propositions of belief as absolutely essential for salvation, one of which was the verbal inspiration of Scripture. They called these propositions the 'fundamentals'. As a self-conscious title, fundamentalism did not emerge until early in the twentieth century and thus marks only one segment of the much longer history of American literalist theology. The title has become largely pejorative and is today replaced by the term 'evangelicalism'.[4]

THE EMERGENCE OF HISTORICAL CRITICISM

It is against the backdrop of this pervasive belief in biblical literalism that the rise of nineteenth century biblical science (called historical criticism) must be seen, if one is to understand the fury and bitterness of the warfare that emerged. This new interpretation of the Bible was guided by sensitive, moral men of faith; but it has to be conceded that, as the literalists never tired of repeating, they did approach the Bible from a perspective totally foreign to that of the literalist. From the perspective of historical criticism **the Bible must be interpreted as would be any other ancient document. It is the product of human creation, depicting human events in which the supernatural, as a miraculous intervention into natural causation, played no role.** There were, of course, many evolving stages in the self-understanding of this developing science. But I think it accurate to say this was the basic presupposition and that at times the conservative theologians saw it more clearly than did the nineteenth century biblical scientists themselves.

The conclusion which the literalist drew from his perception of the presupposition was, however, tragically wrong; namely, that the literal interpreters were atheists and infidels. Whole issues of revelation and transcendence, which have demanded the most sophisticated reasonings of theologians over the centuries, were thus simplistically swept under the rug with the seemingly common sense dictum: It is either God's book or it is worthless. In this respect, the liberals were far closer to the historic faith of the church than were the literalists.

There is no space here to follow the details of the battle that emerged. The fight centered around the Bible, which both claimed as evidence for the correctness of their views. Even the non-biblical issue of Darwinian evolution was related to the Bible's teaching about creation in Genesis one, so that the fight about Darwin and that about the Bible fused into one.

Control over denominational teaching was an inevitable center of combat. As mentioned, the prestigious Princeton Theological Seminary maintained a rigid literalism throughout the nineteenth century and well into the twentieth. On the other hand, the first president of the University of Chicago, William Rainey Harper, was an enthusiastic liberal interpreter of the Old Testament (Funk, pp. 8-11). For him liberal interpretation was a liberating force which would lead to a mature faith in Christianity, not militate against it as the literalists claimed. He created a divinity school faculty of which half were biblical professors. He inaugurated a correspondence course for the study of Hebrew. And, perhaps the best insight into his earnest faith in the Bible as a book for moderns, he became, while president of the university, church school superintendent at the local Baptist church and brought in two New Testament colleagues, one to be superintendent of instruction and the other, director of benevolence (Funk, p. 15).

At Princeton and at Chicago there was no internal opposition to the prevailing views, the one literalist, the other liberal. Nevertheless, a conservative Baptist seminary was created in Chicago to counteract the 'heretical' views espoused at the nominally Baptist divinity school of the university. Liberal Presbyterians teaching elsewhere than at Princeton were harried and hunted. In famous heresy trials, three eminent Presbyterian professors were defrocked, and the famous Harry Emerson Fosdick was apparently saved from censure in his pulpit at the First Presbyterian Church of New York City largely because he was himself a Baptist (Sandeen, pp. 249-52). Even at the Chicago Theological Seminary, which in general seems to have been aligned with Harper's program, there was a witch hunt of sorts. George Holley Gilbert, a productive and competent liberal New Testament professor was, in effect, forced to resign after continued harrassment by conservative alumni and Board members.[5]

In view of the continued intra-denominational battles, it is ironic that the most famous and visible airing of the controversy occurred in a civil law court, namely the Scopes trial in Tennessee in 1925. This bit of Americana is, unfortunately, so well known that I do not need to dwell on it here (Furniss, pp. 3-13). It ended in a Pyrrhic victory for the literalists. Scopes was convicted, but the fundamentalists were discredited in the eyes of most modern Americans.

Perhaps actually most important for the turn of the tide was the fact that the literalists had lost their unceasing attempts to keep liberalism out of the denominations and theological schools. Even Princeton Theological Seminary moved away from its earlier literalist position, a movement which eventually caused the literalists to secede. The decline of strength of the literalists was ironically symbolized by the fact that the final Presbyterian trials were of the secessionists, not the liberals. Fundamentalism, or literalism, seemed to have been thoroughly discredited, its forces routed from the denominations and disorganized. From the liberal perspective, pockets of literalist resistance remained and would likely continue to exist. But there seemed no doubt as to the fact of a final victory for the liberals.

THE CONTEMPORARY SITUATION

It is now clear that there was no such final victory. Indeed a possible new conflict is threatening to emerge, although it can be avoided; and even if it does occur, it will not have the same contours as the earlier battle. The question before us is this: How, if the literalists were discredited and disorganized by the late twenties, have they been able to emerge in the seventies as a powerful force?

Most of the power within the mainline denominations has since the twenties been held by liberals or moderates. The Southern Baptist Convention and the Missouri Synod Lutheran Church (in its most recent manifestation) are partial exceptions. The mainline seminaries were lost to the literalists as well. From their perspective this meant they were being forced out of these institutions. And that left just one solution — to create institutions conducive to their own theology and control. This they proceeded systematically to do.

Within the Presbyterian Church this happened with the formation of Westminster Seminary and the Presbyterian Church of America, the latter being itself soon splintered, with the rightwing millennialists forming the Bible Presbyterian Synod, into whose midst came Carl McIntire. Conservative crusades throughout American colleges and universities were mounted by the Inter-Varsity Christian Fellowship, founded in 1940. To counteract the National Council of Churches, composed of the mainline denominations, the conservatives founded the National Association of Evangelicals and the stricter and more militant American Council of Christian Churches, both in 1941 (Gasper, pp. 21-30). By 1975 the NAE listed 33 affiliated denominations, most of which, however, are quite small in number.

Educational institutions have been established with far greater scope and influence than the old Bible colleges could claim. Wheaton College in Illinois and Westmont College in California are leading undergraduate evangelical institutions. Besides the preeminent Fuller Theological Seminary in California (founded in 1954), Trinity Evangelical Divinity School near Chicago, Gordon-Conwell Theological Seminary in Massachusetts, and Asbury Theological Seminary in Kentucky are important intellectual centers for ministerial training. Dallas Theological Seminary appears to be the national center for dispensationalist seminary training. And, to counteract the liberal tendencies of *The Christian Century* and *Christianity and Crisis* a counter-journal, *Christianity Today*, began to appear in 1956. All this suggests that contemporary evangelicalism has a much stronger and stable power base than its earlier manifestation (Quebedeaux, pp. 18-41).

Furthermore, it also has a much stronger and more able intellectual and theological base. Earlier simplistic and untenable stands on Scripture have been replaced by subtle and sophisticated theological analysis, just as the earlier, in part self-trained, defenders have been replaced by academicians holding degrees froom major centers of theological education. In fact, the word 'literalist' no longer is an adequate label for the thought of many conservatives and should be replaced by a word of their own preference, 'evangelical'. For these thinkers, the notion of the verbal, word-for-word inspiration and literal historical referent funneled through the biblical writers has been discarded. Yet even for them the Bible remains the only source for the Word of God and the notion of the complete inspiration of Scripture is still carefully guarded (Bloesch, pp. 55-59). Furthermore, it can now be affirmed that the **events** narrated by the Bible are the primary saving and revelatory acts of God and are separate from the words of the Bible. What is called 'propositional revelation' is, at least in the system of the moderate evangelical, E. J. Carnell, secondary. He can even state: "To conceive of the Bible as the primary revelation is heresy" (Carnell, p. 49). It is not clear whether even this distinction changes the battlefield, since the Bible alone remains the inspired Word, and since **all** of it is the inspired Word (Carnell, pp. 33, 66). Certainly, however, the weaponry is much more highly sophisticated.

The evangelicals today are thus in a much stronger position than were the fundamentalists of the twenties. If there is to be a new battle, the evangelicals will be much more dangerous opponents.

PROSPECTS AND QUESTIONS FROM A LIBERAL BIAS

Were there space, it would be helpful to trace the exegetical and theological movements within the mainline denominations, since these have been as numerous and important as those within the evangelical churches. Since, however, the conclusion presses in upon me, I can only lift up some hard questions about future prospects for American Christianity as we move beyond the bicentennial year. Are the growing forces of evangelicalism going to force an open battle for the souls of people and for the control of the mainline denominations? One author writing in 1972 put it this way:

> It is not difficult to be pessimistic about the pending schism between liberals and evangelicals in the American church. The signs are everywhere of a disquiet that is growing into open dissent. Positions are hardening. Millions of evangelicals are openly expressing their discontent with the so-called "liberal establishment" in the church. Equally adamant are the liberals who warn that the church must not retreat from its involvement in the crucial socio-political questions of our time (Coleman, p. 13).

This quotation is directed more toward the disagreement over social action, a question I cannot concern myself with here. But the quotation itself is symptomatic of a growing anxiety about open warfare. I confess that I view the prospects of a fight with a certain sense of exhaustion. Personally I do not like to fight, and the language of battle so prominent in this paper is not comfortable to me. For me the issues would seem to have been settled within the long history of theological discussion and within the more recent history of scientific knowledge. I have to say that I feel that my energies should be spent to better and more important tasks of the church than renewing an argument that should have long ago been foreclosed. Nevertheless, no historical prophecy has been accurately guided by an appeal to personal desires. There is no question but that a breakout of the old acrimonious fight between liberals and conservatives may be approaching.

I will cite only one personal example. Recently I gave some lectures to an adult audience at a mainline church in a wealthy suburb of Chicago. My subject necessitated some basic affirmations about critical interpretation of the Gospels. I was immediately and repeatedly, if politely, pressed by two young adults. It was the **older** members of the audience who came to my defense. What had happened was a **reverse** of the usual expectation of young liberals opposing older conservatives. At this church it was old liberals opposing young conservatives.

Thus it is crucial for us to consider the hard questions — and I pose them quite self-consciously from a liberal perspective.

1) Can such a position — the evangelical — maintain itself in the face of the world given us by modern science and philosophy? While the liberal instinctively answers 'no' to this question, the correct answer is clearly 'yes'. All of us have selective eyes and ears; we hear and appropriate what we want to. The fact that most Americans ignore the scientists' plea for more ecological concern leaves no doubt about the fact that people live in compartmentalized worlds. From the presuppositional stance of the evangelical, the compartments he or she builds between science and faith are not inconsistent.

2) Why **would** one choose an evangelical position in preference to that of the liberal? This question requires — and has earned — a book-length treatment (Kelley). The growth of the evangelical churches indicates people are finding something there that is missing in the liberal churches. What they are finding could, of course, be either good or bad, or both. The liberal might too quickly suggest that simple, pat answers and a clear, sharp position are the standard wares of the evangelical churches. But this may be one way of saying that people find **meaning** for life in those churches in distinction from the liberal (Kelley). And it can be said with some justification that the reality affirmed in many liberal congregations is so watered down, so mixed with ordinary secular reality, that it is not clear just what being a liberal Christian **means.** We at least need to consider whether we can affirm a meaning and a reality not identifiable with secular meaning and reality, without falling into the dualistic stance of the evangelical position.

3) Is there not a sociological maxim which indicates that this-generation conservatives are next-generation moderates, thus giving the liberal hope that ultimately the evangelical surge will turn into a surge for the liberal churches? I do not think the liberal can take comfort in this hope. If it is at all true, it will affect only the intellectuals. (This is, admittedly, not to consider other sociological and economic factors.) As long as the liberal position cannot speak to the non-intellectual, the evangelical church will remain strong.

4) If the battle breaks out, will it be as acrimonious as earlier disputes? Hopefully not. Both sides are more secure and more mature than they were seventy-five years ago. Nevertheless, the liberal must remember that the evangelical, by virtue of the extreme stance taken, cannot be as accepting of alternative positions as the liberal. The liberal is not likely to think the evangelical is on the way to damnation (whatever that might mean for the liberal). The evangelical cannot be as sanguine about the future of the liberal.

5) If the battle breaks out, will one side be able to convince the other of its truth? Absolutely not. Each position is working out of a completely different hermeneutical circle and set of presuppositions. This is one of the tragedies of any bitter debate. No one will win, because almost by definition no side can convince the other. The best to be hoped for is earnest but open discussions of each viewpoint for the purpose of better understanding and more acceptance of each other as fellow followers of Jesus.

6) "Shall the evangelicals win?" This is a play on the title of Fosdick's famous sermon, which escalated the fundamentalist attack upon him. As a liberal standing in the latter part of the twentieth century, I honestly do not see how the evangelicals can win, if by 'win' we mean wresting control of the majority of American Christian affections and perhaps even gaining control over the mainline denominations. But I want to conclude with a story which, from the standpoint of the liberal, is perhaps a bit scary.

Yale students in the late eighteenth century had thrown in their lot with the Enlightenment. They were apparently so enthusiastic about the new, rationalistic faith that they assigned each other names of Enlightenment leaders such as Rousseau and Voltaire. They were doubtlessly confident that the world of the Enlightenment, promoted also by such American political figures as Jefferson and Paine, was the world of the future in nineteenth century America. But they were wrong. Timothy Dwight, a confirmed evangelical, appeared on the scene as president of the university, and within a few years the Enlightenment was stamped out. It was replaced by an evangelical revival. What happened at Yale not only was symptomatic of a major religious turn-around for the country as a whole; it actually helped to bring it about (Marsden, pp. 7-10).

Of course the present situation is almost infinitely more complex. But we must nevertheless keep constantly in mind that just because we are **convinced** we know the truth does not mean that our version of the truth wi'll prevail. I do not mean to be an alarmist, much less a prophet; but I do call us to the awareness that truth is ever precariously held and defended. It is never secure and is not always victorious. In these days we must be more open to other visions of truth and yet prepared to defend, if necessary, our own.

NOTES:

1. For a biblical scholar to treat a theme that properly belongs to the realm of American church history is admittedly audacious. In this paper I have drawn together for purposes of reflection the judgments of scholars competent in the field, and am heavily dependent upon the view of those scholars listed in the bibliography. In particular, E. R. Sandeen's *The Roots of Fundamentalism* has been of significant help to me.
2. Alistair Kee, *The Way of Transcendence* (Harmondsworth: Penguin Books, 1971).
3. G. E. Wright, "The Christian Interpreter as Biblical Critic," *Interpretation* I (1947), 135f.
4. Because of space limitations a whole, fascinating dimension of literalism cannot be discussed here, namely that original speculation, claimed to be based on an absolutely literal interpretation of the Bible, called dispensationalism. This was an extreme millennialist position, including novel features such as the 'secret rapture'. Any reader of the popular *Scofield Reference Bible* has come into contact with the basic views of dispensationalism. See Ryrie for a contemporary exposition.
5. A. C. McGiffert, Jr., *No Ivory Tower* (Chicago: The Chicago Theological Seminary, 1965), p. 115.

SUGGESTIONS FOR FURTHER READING:

Bloesch, Donald G., *The Evangelical Renaissance.* (Grand Rapids: Eerdmans, 1973).

Carnell, E. J., *The Case for Orthodox Theology.* (Philadelphia: Westminster, 1959).

Coleman, Richard J., *Issues of Theological Warfare: Evangelicals and Liberals.* (Grand Rapids: Eerdmans, 1972).

Fosdick, Harry E., "Shall the Fundamentalist Win?", *The Christian Century,* June 8, 1922.

The Fundamentals, 10 vols. (Chicago: Testimony, 1910-15).

Funk, Robert W., "The Watershed of the American Biblical Tradition: The Chicago School, First Phase, 1892-1920," *The Journal of Biblical Literature,* 95 (1976), 1-22.

Furniss, Norman F., *The Fundamentalist Controversy, 1918-1931.* (Hamden: Archon, 1963).

Gasper, Louis, *The Fundamentalist Movement.* (The Hague: Mouton, 1963).

Henry, Carl F. H., ed. *Revelation and the Bible.* (Grand Rapids: Baker, 1958).

Kelley, Dean M., *Why Conservative Churches Are Growing.* (New York: Harper, 1972).

Marsden, George M., *The Evangelical Mind and the New School Presbyterian Experience.* (New Haven: Yale, 1970).

Quebedeaux, Richard, *The Young Evangelicals.* (New York: Harper, 1974).

Ryrie, Charles, C., *Dispensationalism Today.* (Chicago: Moody, 1965).

Sandeen, Ernest R., *The Roots of Fundamentalism.* (Chicago: University of Chicago, 1970).

Wells, David and Woodbridge, John, eds., *The Evangelicals.* (Nashville: Abingdon, 1975).

A CONTINENTAL VIEW OF THE AMERICAN EXPERIENCE

By ANDRÉ LACOCQUE

In this year of the bicentennial, colleagues and friends of CTS have asked me for a candid "Continental view of the American experience." I feel humbled by their request, as my only credentials for such an undertaking are that I am a European by birth and a Hebrew Bible student by profession. The latter in particular allows me to criticize what I witness without being personally out of the picture. Were I American by birth, I believe that I would speak no differently, but existentially I might not know events on the European stage, mention of which will occur in what follows. From this point of view, mine is a Continental view, and a very committed one for that matter. But the American experience, however vague the expression, has become my experience; my critique of it is as much directed to myself as to anyone else who cares about what I say here.

Being a theologian, I find one aspect of "the American experience" particularly striking. I think of what Robert Bellah has called "the civil religion" (after Jean-Jacques Rousseau in *The Social Contract*, ch. 8, bk. 4), and which others dub as "general religion," "folk religion," "American Shinto," etc. I want to address this aspect, not only to give vent to my professional taste, but also because it is, I believe, the kingly route toward an understanding in depth of the American experience. I intend therefore to appraise the tenets of American civil religion, and to try their validity from a Judeo-Christian point of view. The question of the existence of other civil religions in history and in the contemporary world will then be dealt with. Finally, the paradigm of Israel for so many civil religionists in this country and elsewhere will be discussed.

A full description of "American civil religion" is impossible here. It is more an ethos than a dogmatic stance. Fortunately for all of us, no Thomas Aquinas wrote a *Summa Theologiae* of the "general religion" of America. Two writers will help us in this descriptive part, a Jewish thinker and a Christian theologian: Will Herberg and Herbert Richardson. But first it seems appropriate to stress an obvious but easily forgotten phenomenon: no tourist, no immigrant, no foreign student coming to this country can miss the pervasive religiosity on the American scene. In our universal post-religious era, attachment to Deism is most remarkable. To a Jewish or Christian apologist, the fact is easily thrilling, encouraging, elating. So, God is not dead, after all. The atheism of the Communists is not triumphant. In the mightiest, "second to none" nation on earth, adjectives which belong to the liturgy of civil religion, "in God we trust" is still unabashedly maintained. The apologist still sees hope for Judaism and Christianity in this world of ours. America appears to him as an appointee of God, as having a "manifest destiny," as a messenger of the divine to all other nations under the sky. The American civil religion is not only for private circulation, it is also eschatologically universal. Its tenets, however, are a strange mixture of Judeo-Christian affirmations and humanistic principles permeated with idealism and moralism. To the belief in an anonymous Being is added an unshakable faith in education, and, more profoundly, in man's natural goodness and perfectibility. It is an optimistic religion, a religion of well-fed people, inclined to believe that problems can and will be solved, that we shall not always have the poor with us, that there are righteous people around, even many of them, especially in America. It is also, of course, a triumphant religion, a successful and success-oriented philosophy. More specifically, it is a shared set of beliefs in the **individual's** ability to make his place in the sun. Thanks to birth control and to somewhat effective rules on immigration, there is enough room for many, if not for all.

Will Herberg confirms this view of ours.[1] Herbert Richardson goes deeper.[2] To him, association of "civil" and "religion" suggests: 1) the affirmation "that this group has a transcendent goal and some ultimate value;" 2) "the categories of politics, sovereignty, law, justice, **the state,** are especially appropriate for describing ultimate reality." Richardson continues his analysis saying, " . . . in analogizing we not only ascribe finite characteristics to what is infinite, we also claim infinite characteristics for what is finite." In other words, the theological   problem raised by civil religion is not in the use or misuse of it by people, but in the very essence of religion being civil or acculturated . . . whenever . . . we seek to relate American politics to God's sovereignty, we are also relating God's sovereignty to American politics. In attempting to be pious, we can also become proud."

The association of civil religion with the political, i.e., with the welfare of the "civitas" or the "polis," has been stressed by Sydney Mead, a definite supporter of that kind of religion. Mead rightly draws a parallel with the "Christian" Roman Empire "combining elements of Platonism with the tenets of Stoics."[3] Although this situation may please a humanitarian, it is doubtful whether this religion of man (which unavoidably led to the cult of the first man of the Empire, viz. the Emperor) will leave the theologian unconcerned. True, there is no American Emperor, but there does seem to be an American imperium. The substitution of a pluralistic cult for an individualistic one is not, however, without grave questions. Moreover, Richard Nixon has recently demonstrated that the gap between these two cults is easily filled. Blatant misuse of civil religion is virtually an inherent part of it. I shall try to demonstrate this later.

Earlier in this article, we saw that the main characteristic of folk religion is belief in an anonymous Supreme Being. It may be that in the mind of millions of Americans, God is the Judeo-Christian "Lord," but He does not need to be named, lest civil religion become "provincial" or "sectarian". Sydney Mead is enthusiastic about religion precisely because of its "cosmopolitanism." Benjamin Franklin spoke of it as encapsulating "the essentials of every religion." Here we touch the very root of American pluralism. All peculiarities are tolerated **as idiosyncrasies.** Be your God Jehovah, the Father of Christ, Jupiter, Marduk, Satan, the Great Manitu, deified ancestors, or the American nation is irrelevant. The general has swallowed the particular, like philanthropy swallows the love of my neighbor. Dwight Eisenhower expressed it in a blunt "military" way when he declared that the United States needs to be bolstered by a religion "and I don't care what it is."[4]

In fact, Eisenhower was right not to care. He intuited that the ambiguity of civil religion's "God" was self resolving. I mean that what is true in all religions,[5] even when the gods are invoked by their names, is still truer in a religion which does not specify the object of its faith: ultimately man himself, on the individual level, or the nation, on the communal level is the recipient of worship. J. Paul Williams[6] has shown that in America, Democracy has become a religion as in ancient Rome, "vox populi, vox Dei." One is stunned (at least, I am stunned) to learn that the great Abraham Lincoln on February 11, 1861, in Indianapolis, cried out, "When the people rise in masses in behalf of the Union and the liberties of our country, truly may it be said, 'The gates of hell shall not prevail aginst them'"[7] In a religion of patriotism where "national life is apotheosized, national values religionized, national heroes are divinized, national history is experienced as a **Heilsgeschichte**, as a redemptive history" (Will Herberg), one is somewhat suspicious as to the meaning of John F. Kennedy's words (or at least their revealing order) when he said, "I have sworn before you and the Almighty God." Others were less ambiguous; Eisenhower declared, "America is great, because she is good." The President had just spoken of America as the mightiest power ever. Richard Nixon carried the idolatry further. In a book on *The Nixon Theology*,[8] Charles B. Henderson, Jr. writes: "Nixon systematically appropriates the vocabulary of the church, faith, trust, hope, belief, spirit, and applies these words not to

74

a transcendent God but to his own nation, and worse, to his personal vision of what that nation should be . . . Lacking a transcendent God, he seems to make partiotism his religion, the American dream his deity." Nixon is not an isolated case. Were it not for the **revelation** of Watergate, he would still be in power, plebiscited by "the silent majority." The God of civil religion is purely utilitarian, maintained on a man-made pedestal for pragmatic reasons. Washington was candidly explicit: "Of all the dispositions and habits which lead to political prosperity, Religion and Morality are indispensable supports."[9] Such a God is viewed as having a special concern for America and, hence, "clashes" so to speak with the Judeo-Christian God who, we are told, is in a covenantal relationship with another people, Israel. Jefferson's second inaugural address overcame the difficulty in "naturalizing" Him. "I shall need, too, the favor of that Being in whose hands we are, who led our fathers, as Israel of old, from their native land and planted them in a country flowing with all the necessaries and comforts of life." Sydney Mead[10] comments on this saying, "Europe is Egypt; America, the promised land. God has led his people to establish a new sort of social order that shall be a light unto all the nations." As a reminder, that very equation of America with "Israel of old" has been used as a slogan for the destruction of the native Indians. It is today used the same way in South Africa to justify the apartheid.

This point deserves full consideration. Abraham Lincoln himself spoke of Americans as an "almost chosen people." Soon enough the "almost" was dropped. John E. Smylie[11] writes: " . . . the nation (U.S.) emerged as the primary agent of God's meaningful activity in history." The corrosive illusion is entertained among Americans that they are under the holy obligation to carry out God's will on earth. It is their "manifest destiny." It is their sacred duty to eradicate evil from nations plunged in darkness. Secretly or overtly it is believed that all social systems different from the American way of life are forced upon other nations. Only we see the light, and must make it visible to all. Such a Messianistic conception entails an intolerable complacency which is not without irritation to many abroad. We shall come back to this point later.

If space permitted, we might explore further the issue of America as the new Israel. Suffice it here to recall that Yahwism was **not** a state religion, or a civil religion, except perhaps during the short period of the Reform under Ezra and Nehemiah, when the Judeans were a minute population lost in the immensity of the Persian empire and could not possibly have any imperialistic expansionist views. There have been, it is true, times of temptation along that line in Israel. History keeps with horror the memory of such a "fall" in the days of King Jehu of Israel. The parallel with American civil religion is sometimes striking. Jehu became the champion of Jehovah. In his time and under his next successors (Jeroboam II in particular) Yahwism became a state religion. It seems that the word "Baal" itself became taboo. The book of Amos does not even mention it once. But Jehu and Jeroboam did not remain unchallenged by God's prophets. Amos and Hosea denounce the hoax. They use the strongest words in the Hebrew language to express the disgust of their Lord. Israel is not a radiant bride, she is a whore. She is not a faithful wife, endowed with a sacred mission to the nations, and blessed "with all the necessaries and comforts of life," she is doomed to utter destruction.

To the student of Israel's history, the recurrent claims of one nation after another to "chosenness" are staggeringly one-sided. What the nations unilaterally chose to understand under the concept of election is privilege, never the impossible mission of a ceaseless martyrdom. All are willing to be "the light of the nations" but without the Suffering Servant. All wish they were Abraham, but without Morijah. All feel they are Messianic, but without the cross of Calvary. Or rather, the Suffering Servant, the Morijah trial, the Cross, are transferred to the Jews, and to all those whom it is convenient to assimilate with the Jews: the Negroes, the Indians, the Chicanos, the Vietnamese, the Communists, and so forth. Civil religion is in theory universalistic, but practically it is strictly "elitist". Blacks, Indians, Jews, and dogs are not welcome!

Thus, all the elements are gathered which lean dangerously toward Fascism. In this year of the bicentennial of our nation, it is urgent that we realize the abysmal pit in which this country can be engulfed. As a witness of the European thirties and forties, my "Continental view" can perhaps become prophetic. Nothing is more ominous than naive self-complacency. French arrogance in the thirties was monstrous. People were boasting that they would annihilate Germany in a week, maybe two at the most. Their complex of superiority knew no restraint. At that time a book was published under the title: *Dieu est-il français?* (*Is God French?*). The "manifest destiny" of France was unquestioned because unquestionable. All other nations, Germany first, were still living in barbarian Middle-Ages. Meanwhile, beyond the border, the situation was still worse. The French were sure of the rectitude of their ideas and ideals, but Hitler taught his nation that ideas and ideals were the direct outcome of blood-quality. Other nations **could** not think right, feel right, act right, because the impurity of their non-Aryan blood prevented them from such nobility. Therefore, Germans **could** not be wrong; the quality of their blood, their very substance made it impossible for them to be wrong. Germany was great because she was good, period. The enemies were those, in the first place the Jews, who dared question the German **Geist** and thus endanger the embodiment of **Geist**, i.e., the German **Kultur**. [12] Ethics stemmed from the self. The greatest achievement was to be unabashedly German, to be unequivocally and without restraint proud of the self. The "Supreme

Being," in a very convenient metaphor, had appointed Germany and her Fuhrer as the new Israel (again!) for a new world order. **Gott** was **mit uns**; better still, **Gott** was **uns.** If there has been some trace of genius in Adolf Hitler, for it takes at least some semblance of genius to be so perfectly a buffoon, it expressed itself in presenting to the nation a religious image of themselves without the thin coat of Judeo-Christian paint. Hitler demonstrated that 2000 years of Christianity in the Western world has not eliminated the roots of paganism. It does not take much to unearth them and to awake the dormant paganism of our peoples.

There are two reasons why this happens. One is the non-demagogical character of Judeo-Christianity, its refusal to put man in the center, or, if you will, its demand for absolute oblation to God. The second reason is a variation of the first, and will allow us to go into more depth: to avoid being under the demand of the impossible, nations have reduced Judeo-Christianity to the level of a **religion.** Religion, from the Latin **religere,** to bind again, is the human effort to bridge the gap between oneself and God, The religious enterprise starts with **man** and climbs up step by step the ladder towards God. The biblical metaphor of the Tower of Babel aptly expresses the Promethean human attempt to reach the divine — not for love of the divine, but for becoming the divine, "You shall be like gods." This the religious man achieves by accumulating victories, successes, virtues, performances, good feelings, clean conscience, unparalleled power, self-congratulations, Memorial Days, bicentennial displays of national "ego-trips." True, religion yields phenomena and feelings which can be confused with those of the Judeo-Christian faith. For a while the crowd on Mount Carmel may consider Elijah and the Baal charlatans equally as prophets. Their vocabulary to a certain extent at least is similar, and they both have recourse to prayer and to oracle. Indeed, the quality of spectacle is often higher with the "prophets" of Baal (cf. 1 Kings 18:26 ff.). Nazi meetings on the central square of Nuremberg surrounded by the majestic Alps were infinitely more elating than the "cold" worship services in the local churches. If really we are after ". . . a deeply felt religious faith . . . and I don't care what it is," our choice is made. If what is important is not to praise the Creator, but to flatter the creature, if it is to build up muscles as "the mightiest nation on earth" with the evident blessing of the "Supreme Being," then the prophetic calls to repent appear incongruous and insane. Such "particularism" is obsolete, such a God is too petty. "Religion "offers a vague and empty "god," playing the convenient role of blessing our arsenal, of being present when needed, and not being present when he understands that discretion is required of him. Such a god embraces all and everything, as long as its components are without substance. His names emphasize his anonymity and facelessness; he is "patriotism," "democratic system," "the American

Dream," "America, America." His flag beside communion tables in temples and churches underlines his tragic absence. For that nameless god is Idol. It lends itself to the shapes of our whims, a fact which does not awaken our suspicion, for we call it "pluralism." It is an "it," and as such it is a comfortable, kaleidoscopic image of our vague yearnings. It does not speak; men, and especially its High Priests, the Presidents of the United States, speak for it, again a very convenient virtue of the Idol. But be not mistaken, it can require incredible sacrifices. Only Jehovah halts the hand of the sacrificing father; Moloq being a machine must be fed with our children.

Some critics try to draw parallels with Israel's "civil religion." Even a good theologian such as Herbert Richardson, embarrassed as he is with the analogies drawn by American civil religion with Old Testament categories, thinks discarding the model is appropriate. The New Testament "seeks to displace the political-legal model of ultimate reality (proposed by the Old Testament) . . . the 'gospel' is that which liberates us from the 'law,'" etc. Forgotten in the process is that Israel is not religious. In fact she is the greatest anti-religious enterprise ever. Religion has always been and will always be bound to Nature. J. Paul Williams[13] typically writes that democratic ideal is "the will of God, or, if they please, of Nature." Religion is an accumulation; Israel's faith is a becoming. Martin Marty pinpoints what we are speaking about when, describing the identity of the American god, he says: "In any case he or it represents a promissor to the nation."[14] In other words, religion is without a sense of sin and judgment. Senator Mark Hatfield understands well the impassable chasm between religion and faith: "If we as leaders appeal to the god of civil religion, our faith is in a small and exclusive deity, a loyal spiritual advisor to power and prestige, a defender of only the American nation, the object of a national folk religion devoid of moral content. But if we pray to the biblical God of justice and righteousness, we fall under God's judgment for calling upon his name but failing to obey his commands."[15] The point for faith in "the biblical God of justice and righteousness" is not, as in civil religion, to correct some mistakes, to straighten some deviations, to smooth some edges. The point is not to propose some therapeutic for modern illnesses, or to cultivate some potential religiosity in the nation. If anything, Israel's prophets proclaimed that the malady is beyond healing (Isaiah 1), that all religiousness is harlotry (Hosea), that all mystical elation is a dance before the golden calf or the golden eagle. They tore down all the religious. Their living God loathed sacrifices, the trampling of the Temple threshold, church songs, Memorial Days, the cult of national heroes . . . everything purporting to make man "feel good," that is, feel at ease with his conscience, guiltless, sinless.

In this bicentennial time, we need Israel's prophets to unmask all the injustices at home and abroad. They have been condoned by a religiously based conviction that the poor and oppressed **deserve** their fate, because God is not with them as He is with us. Civil religion has turned God's challenge to our riches into self-congratulation. It sees Job as guilty of some hidden, terrible crime, whose gravity is the yardstick of his predicament. We, his "friends," have the religious chivalry to come to his rescue with our dollars, provided it is understood that he is wrong and we are right. There is room in generous America for relenting Jobs. So speaks civil religion. But after Dresden, Hiroshima and Nagasaki, after My Lai abroad; after the concentration camps for U.S. Japanese, the race for atomic weapons, the insane exploitation of the world's riches, the ineptness of churches to transcend racial differences in their own areas, after the unctuousness of Rabbi Edgar F. Magnin and the Rev. Billy Graham, after Watergate, it has become obscene to give free reign to our arrogance.

For a nation's worth is not measured by its natural riches, nor by the might it can marshall to intimidate other nations. True, such a display of power succeeds for a time in imposing awe on less privileged peoples. But the price paid is the contempt in which the U.S. is held in the whole world. The prophets have taught us that the cries of the oppressed cannot remain unanswered.

This view of the American civil religion is not, I contend, a mere "Continental view." As I already indicated, I would hold the same language were I born in this country. Moreover, my critique does not emanate from "outside." It is both the expression of my love for this country and of my trust in its capacity to receive criticisms and to reform its ways. The very fact that I can without fear write this article is the greatest homage one can pay to America. As Golda Meir recently said: "There is a very simple criterion for probing the democratic institutions of a nation, you just ask: Where is your opposition? In the parliament or in jail?"

NOTES:

1.   *American Civil Religion*, ed. by Russell E. Richey and Donald G. Jones, (New York: Harper and Row, 1974), pp. 76 ff.
2.   *Ibid.* pp. 161 ff.
3.   *Ibid.* p. 47.
4.   Quoted by Will Herberg, *Protestant, Catholic, Jew*, (Garden City, N.Y.: Anchor Books, 1960), p. 97.
5.   In this article, the term "religion" does not apply to Israel. I shall show why hereafter.
6.   J. Paul Williams, *What Americans Believe and How They Worship*, (New York: Harper and Bros., 1952).
7.   Quoted by Sydney Mead, *The Lively Experiment* (New York: Harper and Row, 1963), p. 68.

8. New York 1972, p. 193.
9. Farewell Address.
10. *The Lively Experiment, op. cit.* p. 12.
11. *Christianity Today*, XX, October 1963, p. 314.
12. Nazism spoke of *Kultur*, not of civilization. Culture is static, a heritage of generations. Civilization is much more imponderable, an aim, a future, a telos. There is conceivably an Israelite civilization, but hardly an Israelite culture.
13. *What Americans Believe . . .*, p. 71.
14. *American Civil Religion*, p. 145.
15. Quoted in *The Christian Century*, Feb. 21, 1973, p. 221.

THE AMERICAN JEWISH EXPERIENCE

By RABBI ROBERT J. MARX

The American Jewish experience can best be described in terms of an ongoing struggle between piety and polity, between the demands of God and synagogue on the one hand, and the social, political and human needs of immigrant generations on the other.

Unlike most other immigrant groups, the Jewish experience with America was multi-faceted and multi-generational. The process began with Jews of Sephardic or Spanish background who came to New Amsterdam, as early as 1654, and was followed by widely-spaced waves of immigration — from Germany in the 1840s, from Russia and Eastern Europe in the last decades of the nineteenth century and early decades of the twentieth, again from Germany in the Hitler days of the 1930s and 40s and finally, though on a reduced scale, with immigrants again from Russia in the 1970s. In all of these migrations, the newcomers experienced, and the older settlers reexperienced the meaning of alienation, of relocation, and of the need to be helped and to help. Whether there was an ambivalent love-hate attitude as was exhibited by the Sephardim toward the German-Jewish immigrants in the 1840s and more intensely by the German Jews toward their Russian coreligionists in the late decades of the nineteenth century, or whether there was an unconditional desire to help, the existing Jewish community was deeply affected by the new waves of immigration. There were moments of heroic self-sacrifice, as when the Jewish community rallied to save the victims of Nazism and to offer them a haven in a land which was not to comprehend their horror until six million had died. There were also embarrassing responses to the plight of their coreligionists, the resolution, for example, passed by the Board of Managers of the Associated Hebrew Charities of Chicago in the year 1886, stating: "That we condemn the transportation of paupers into this country and Canada by European societies... All such as are unable to maintain themselves should be forthwith returned whence they came."[1]

The Jewish immigrants to America brought with them many things, but most poignantly they brought with them their memories — memories of their communities in the old country, memories of lighting Sabbath candles at home, memories of Rosh Hashanah and Yom Kippur — memories of God. Their memories were, at the best, to be changed in America, at the worst, distorted by the realities they found here. And yet, always the memories even after five generations, were, for those who remained, both a problem and a challenge.

In the earliest days of immigration, the major thrust of Jewish energy was spent in being accepted, in becoming like everyone else. But becoming like everyone else, except for those who abandoned their faith, had to be achieved in the context of one's Jewishness. Thus, as early as 1655, Asser Levy, a Jewish immigrant to New Amsterdam, insisted that he had as much right to serve in Peter Stuyvesant's militia as did any non-Jew.[2]

Nor were Jews immune to the secular stresses and strains of life in a new land. Dr. Jacob Marcus describes to us the anguish of one of those early pioneers, Michael Judah, who came to Connecticut in colonial days and tried to save his family "Jewishly." He could save himself but not his child:

> He stubbornly persisted, living and dying as a Jew. Among the articles found in his pitifully meager inventory of belongings was a "killing knive," certainly a *halif* used by the shohet in slaughtering animals. Apparently he attempted to provide himself with kosher meat and poultry. In his will he left his son, David, five pounds. Was this the bulk of his possessions? Or is it too far fetched to assume that he was dissatisfied with this his only child, his circumcised son, David, who had moved to Fairfield, married a Gentile, and had broken completely with the traditions of the fathers? Michael left his estate to the Jewish people of New York: one half to the synagogue and the other half to the poor widows and orphans of the community.[3]

From a secular point of view the problem was clear — survive! The challenge was always tremendous and the odds were overwhelming. The German settlers in the 1840s were characteristically peddlers. They purchased some dry goods, put packs on their backs and moved to the West. The cities of the Ohio Valley and the Midwest became their homes. Pittsburgh, Cincinnati, St. Louis, Cleveland, Chicago became new Jewish centers. The new settlers built homes and synagogues. Their children were to become the professionals of the Jewish community. They were to become doctors and lawyers, social workers and teachers.

In every city where sizable numbers of German Jews settled, there was a synagogue. The old faith held its power. But there were strange modifications to the ancient faith. Reform was the religious mood of the day — in Germany and in the United States. The service these German Jews instituted was not the service of the old, traditional synagogue. The service was conducted in English, men and women sat together, a choir took the place of the traditional *chazan* or cantor. The thrust was twofold: Keep Judaism for the young. Make it a religion congenial to America.

Coming to Albany, New York, in 1845, Isaac M. Wise reveals in his *Reminiscences* the problems and the anguish of building a religious community in a new land. Wise was later to move to Cincinnati where he founded not only the Union of American Hebrew Congregations and the Hebrew Union College, but also the Central Conference of American Rabbis, the central organization of the reform rabbinate. In his spare time, Wise served as full-time rabbi of a large congregation and edited a newspaper.

Who were the people Isaac M. Wise served? Early in his *Reminiscences*, Wise tells of a strange encounter he had with one of his closest friends:

> One afternoon I met on the street a man with a large, old straw hat drawn far over his face. He was clad in a perspired linen coat, and carried two large tin boxes on his shoulders. He had a large clay pipe in his mouth, a pair of golden spectacles on his nose, and dragged himself along with painful effort. I looked at him closely, and recognized my friend Stein. Upon noticing my astonishment, he said, smilingly: "Most of the German and Polish Jews in America look like this, and the rest of them did till a very short time ago." As he was going homeward I accompanied him to his house. A quarter of an hour later he emerged completely metamorphosed. He looked genteel again. He informed his wife laughingly that I had met him in his peddler's costume. He now described to me graphically the misery and the drudgery of the peddler's life. Our people in this country, said he, may be divided into the following classes: (1) the basket-peddler — he is as yet altogether dumb and homeless; (2) the trunk carrier, who stammers some little English, and hopes for better times; (3) the pack-carrier, who carries from one hundred to one hundred and fifty pounds upon his back, and indulges the thought that he will become a business man some day. In addition to these, there is the aristocracy, which may be divided into three classes: (1) The wagon-baron, who peddles through the country with a one or two horse team; (2) the jewelry-count who carries a stock of watches and jewelry in a small trunk, and is considered a rich man even now; (3) the store-prince, who has a shop, and sells goods in it. At first one is the slave of the basket or the pack; then the lackey of the horse, in order to become finally the servant of the shop.[4]

Isaac M. Wise was not to have an easy time in Albany. Two days before Rosh Hashanah one year, his congregation voted him out of office. Advised by the Attorney General and his friends that he ought to perform his official duties, Wise resolved to confront the congregation and its president, Louis Spanier. Here is the scene on the morning of that holy occasion as Wise described it.

> I went to the synagogue on New Year's morning, appeared in my official garb, but found one of Spanier's creatures, who had been the cause of the altercation about the Sabbath, sitting in my chair. I took another seat. Excitement ruled the hour. Everything was quiet

as the grave. Finally the choir sings Sulzer's great *En Komokho.* At the conclusion of the song I step before the ark in order to take out the scrolls of the law as usual, and to offer prayer. Spanier steps in my way, and, without saying a word, smites me with his fist so that my cap falls from my head. This was the terrible signal for an uproar the like of which I have never experienced. The people acted like furies. It was as though the synagogue had suddenly burst forth into a flaming conflagration. The Poles and Hungarians, who thought only of me, struck out like wild men. The young people jumped down from the choir-gallery to protect me, and had to fight their way through the surging crowd. Within two minutes the whole assembly was a struggling mass. The sheriff and his posse, who were summoned, were belabored and forced out until finally the whole assembly surged out of the house into Herkimer Street. 'Louis Spanier,' said I to him, 'there is the law to which I can appeal.' 'I have a hundred thousand dollars more than you. I do not fear the law. I will ruin you.' I finally reached home, bowed with pain and inexpressible grief. The constable came and arrested me as the ringleader of a rebellious mob at a public service.[5]

What did Isaac M. Wise do? He and his followers created a new congregation in Albany. We see in Wise's description of the new synagogue the spirit which underlined the new religious thrust of the German Reformers. Reform Judaism was to be the religion of America. It would be modern enough and appealing enough to attract the young. It would be accessible to everyone — Jews and non-Jews alike.

The day of dedication arrived finally. Dr. Lilienthal was invited to deliver the German oration, in order to give me the opportunity to explain to the world in English the significance of the new movement in Judaism. The choir had rehearsed for two months. Everything was in readiness, all state and city officials were invited. The scholars and literati of the library; in truth, all the most prominent people of the city were present when the new temple, in all its splendor and glory, was dedicated as a Jewish house of worship. It was a day of ecstatic enthusiasm for us, an hour of atonement and heartfelt *rapprochement* between the Jews and the most cultured non-Jews of the city of Albany.[6]

How different was the thrust of the East European immigrants who began arriving thirty years after Isaac Wise wrestled with Louis Spanier. The expansion of America toward the West had largely been achieved. The Russians settled largely in the cities of the East coast. Their initial choice of a career, too, was different. Whereas the German Jews began their odyssey as peddlers, the Russians began as factory workers. Their religious outlook was intensely Orthodox or else hostile to Judaism altogether. And so the new immigrants starting about 1880 began to establish scores of small shuls or synagogues in every community where they were to be found. Synagogues and workmen's circles, these were the religious and secular symbols of the new immigrants.

Again the struggle to survive and succeed created all kinds of ambivalence.　Hester Street and Delancy Street and Chicago's West Side became living symbols of the Jewish encounter with America in the 1890s. Louis Borgenicht was more than typically successful in a way and yet his story as told by Irving Howe, reveals the cultural tension and psychological trauma faced by the immigrant from Eastern Europe.

Borgenicht and his wife came to America in 1888, lived in an eight-dollar-a-month apartment, and peddled sundries--anything he could buy for a nickel and sell for a dime: herring, notebooks, fruit, socks.

> A driven man, he understood that step-by-step improvements in income would never bring him to the place he dreamed of. He walked the streets, studying what people were wearing and what was being sold in stores, until one day he noticed a little Slavic girl with an apron utterly common in Central Europe but still unknown in America. This, thought Borgenicht, might be the item to make his fortune.

> He bought 150 yards of material in a Hester Street store, and, with the help of his wife, he manufactured forty children's aprons in one day. Within three hours he had sold them all, realizing a profit of $2.60. He then invested all his remaining capital in gingham and white goods, and he and his wife labored six days a week from seven in the morning until late into the night, converting uncut material into enough aprons for him to peddle from house to house. Soon an eighteen-year-old apprentice was hired for six dollars a week. A bit later the Borgenichts rented a store on Sheriff Street and lived in its back rooms. Then a few girls were hired to work on machines in the store. In 1890, two years after his arrival, Borgenicht gave up peddling and concentrated on the manufacture of children's dresses. By 1892 twenty girls were employed in the back room of a large store, with dresses being sold to Bloomingdale's and Ridley Brothers.

Despite his success Borgenicht felt frustrated, unfulfilled, even though by 1913 he was employing 1,500 workers and had surrounded himself with the lavish luxury that material wealth brings. He continued contact with his Jewish culture, served on boards of synagogues, maintained a kosher home, and read Yiddish papers. But his style of life gradually changed, for he wanted to be more like his *hochwohlegeboren* coreligionists in dress, speech, and manners. He was torn between two worlds, that created by his wealth and that of the pietistic culture out of which he had come. He was visibly a success, but perhaps a stranger even to himself.[7]

Of course, not all Jews were as materially successful as Louis Borgenicht. There was the drudgery of the sweat shop, the crowded loneliness of the ghetto. Writes Oscar Handlin,

> In all matters the New World made the peasant less a man. Often he toiled at intangibles, labored to produce objects he never would see. In the laborer's perspective, the factory turned out only parts of things: not a shoe, a coat, a plow, a cart — but a sole, a sleeve, a blade, a wheel. Bound to the monotony of a minute task, endlessly

> repeated, the worker sometimes could not envisage the whole of
> which his bit would be a part. He through whose hands all of
> production had then passed, from the dropped seed to the eaten
> bread, often now could not tell what manner of thing his labor made
> — its shape, its quality, its function. Such labor was labor for its
> own sake and meaningless.[8]

That both the synagogue and the family suffered in the Jewish encounter with America is clear. Jews traditionally pride themselves on the purity of the family and the strength of family ties. With the growing pace of assimilation, however, it is apparent that the same stresses which beset American families in general have not left the Jewish family unscathed. Not only have divorces been on the increase but intermarriage, which has historically been perceived as a threat to the purity of the Jewish family, has increased dramatically in the last several decades. It is now estimated that in the year 1976, over 36% of the Jewish marriages will be between Jews and members of another faith. Although most rabbis still refuse to officiate at mixed marriages, and all of the official rabbinic bodies refuse to condone it, those rabbis who defy their colleagues' opinions and officiate at such weddings, are overwhelmed with requests for their services.

The increasing disruption of the family has led the Jewish community to reexamine its family services with an eye to more effective counseling and to explore alternate life styles for Jews — including the establishment of congregations and Havurot or communes for single people.

Several years ago, I visited a meeting of Alcoholics Anonymous. An acquaintance came up to me and gushed: "Rabbi, when I joined Alcoholics Anonymous, there were only three Jewish members. Now there are seventy-five. Isn't it marvelous?" It is apparent that despite strong family and moral ties, Jews are subject to all of the pathologies of modern civilization.

Where is it then, that Jews in the American experience maintain a uniqueness, if not a separateness? It is in their uses of memory. Let me illustrate the vital role of memory by pointing to the recent reaction on the part of the Jewish community to the United Nations resolution equating Zionism with racism. No action on the part of a world body could have been more calculated to bring terror into Jewish hearts than such an equation. The resolution, on the surface so absurd, is actually a perversion of the Jewish nightmare. Hitler was able to kill Jews by creating a climate in which they were regarded as racially inferior. It was racism, then, that gave impetus to the Zionist idea and the feeling on the part of Jews that they needed a home of their own where they would be free of racism. Hitler, as Hannah Arendt has pointed out so brilliantly, was able to convince his people that being Jewish was not only a crime, it was a disease. Crime could be punished, but disease had to be exterminated.[9] It was the memory of Hitler that made the United Nations' action so horrifying to

Jews just as earlier memories of pogroms in Russia and Poland had evoked Jewish sympathy with the growing effort to establish a homeland in Palestine in the early decades of the twentieth century.

In a strange way, then, memory serves to bring together the polarities of Jewish life, religion and Zionism and religion and secularism. Actually, despite the presence of religious Zionism, Judaism and Jewish nationalism could be expected to confront one another in a hostile way. Judaism represents spirituality, other worldliness, prophetic morality and the dominion of God. Zionism represents nationalism, the exercise of political power and the dominion of the state. Religion emphasizes time. The state emphasizes space. One emphasizes eternity, the other, the land and what is on it. The warning which Samuel gave to his people when they asked him to appoint a king is just as relevant to the modern religionist as it was to the children of Israel 3,000 years ago. The modern state, like the ancient monarchy, faces the charge: "He will take your sons and appoint them for himself, for his chariots, and to be his horsemen, and some shall run before his chariots, and he will appoint him captains over thousands and captains over fifties, and he will set them to plow his ground and to reap his harvest, and to make his instruments of war, and instruments of his chariots."[10] The ancient prophet foresaw the danger of the military state as clearly as the most prescient of our modern day anti-bureaucrats.

Yet it is memory that has bridged the gap between Jewish religious commitment and Jewish nationalism. No Jew feels confident that his memories, his nightmares may not be repeated in some modern context and so the support of Israel becomes a vital part of the modern Jewish experience.

In the 1880s, these memories had not yet coalesced into a uniting force in the Jewish community. The theological changes which have taken place between then and now dramatize just how important a factor these memories have become. In the 1870s, most American Jews were still Sephardic and German. The great religious need as we have pointed out, was to create a form of Judaism that would both accommodate the new American way of life and encourage Jews to remain Jews. Assimilation was a tremendous problem. The Jews of America could still dream, as did Isaac M. Wise, that there could be a Union of American Hebrew Congregations. The name itself was significant. Wise did not envision a union of Reform congregations or a union of Orthodox congregations, but a union of all congregations. Today this is the name by which the Reform segment of Judaism is known, but back in 1873, when Wise created the Union of American Hebrew Congregations, he could dream that all Jews would be united under one banner. (In 1881, only 8 out of 200 synagogues in the United States were Orthodox.[11])

The East European immigrations of the following four decades crushed that hope and served to emphasize the differences between Reform Judaism with its liberal thrust and Orthodox Judaism with its emphasis on one revelation at Mount Sinai in which the entire Torah was revealed to Moses. Conservative Judaism, and later an offshoot of Conservatism, Reconstructionism, stood between the two extremes, recognizing the need for change while maintaining that Reform had gone too far in "Protestantizing" Judaism.

It is always incredible to note how much pessimism has historically surrounded analyses of Jewish survival in the United States. One would think in reading the documents of surveys that Judaism as an organized religion is about to collapse. In 1935, for instance, a survey was made of the young people in New York City. Every tenth person between the ages of 15 and 35 was asked about his or her attendance at religious services. 72% of the men and 78% of the women had not attended a single religious service during the past year. Jewish students, the survey showed, had moved further from their religion than had Catholics and Protestants, and yet, in these "pre-historic" days, the roots of Jewish education were deep. Probably two-thirds to three-fourths of Jewish children received some Jewish education, and not only weekend religious schools, but classes in Yiddish and community-wide Boards of Jewish Education were flourishing.[12] It was as if Judaism was determined to survive in spite of itself.

It was still possible in 1885 for Reform Jews, assembled at a historic conference in Pittsburgh, to adopt a Platform of Belief in which the national uniqueness of Judaism was deemphasized in favor of Americanism and universalism. The Pittsburgh Platform said for example: We no longer consider ourselves a nation, but a religious community. America is our home, not Palestine. Ceremonies and Hebrew are to be deemphasized. Morality and universalism are to be elevated. In other words, what is good is what makes us more American.[13] The Kantian emphasis upon religion as primarily a force for morality was seen by the Reform rabbis as entirely consistent with their understanding of the modern meaning of Judaism.

The advent of Hitler severely challenged the universalism of the reformers. After Hitler, the uniqueness, rather than the universalism of Judaism became the cornerstone of Jewish commitment. There was a growing recognition that all Jews, even if they did not share the same faith, shared the same fate. There was a feeling that Jews had to return to their religious roots. No longer was the Hebrew content of the service reduced. Reform synagogues found themselves moving toward Conservatism and Orthodoxy in terms of increased ritual, Sabbath evening candle lighting and the sanctification of wine, classes in Hebrew for adults as well as children and a new interest in the people and State of Israel. Anti-Semitism and Israel were the two issues that could invariably be counted upon to coalesce the Jewish community.

While ultra-Orthodox Jews still insist that Zion cannot be restored until the Messiah arrives, and the American Council for Judaism, at the other extreme, insists that nationalism has no place in Judaism which it defines religiously, the vast majority of Jews maintain a strange alliance between religion and the State of Israel. Prick Israel and the Jewish community bleeds. But there are some problems. Religious Jews, in increasing numbers, are perplexed by the secularism to be found in Israel and are beginning to ask embarrassing questions about the religious nature of the dialogue between church and state.

Nevertheless, there is a passionate feeling, even on the part of those who might like to see Israel take a more dovish military posture, that Israel represents the one sure hope for the Jewish body if not for the Jewish soul. 2,000 years of homelessness find their redemption in the new state.

If there is a non-holy (though, not necessarily unholy) alliance between Judaism and Zionism, there is an even more problematic dialogue between the secularists and the religionists. Judaism, as has been so often noted, is not a religion. It is a way of life. Its traditions, its laws and institutions encompass every phase of human existence. For the religious Jew, every action, every thought is suffused by the presence and teachings of God. At the same time, vast numbers of Jews feel that philanthropy rather than religion is the cornerstone upon which the Jewish life rests.

In a very real sense, the secular institutions of Jewish life developed out of the Jewish memory, just as did the religious convictions. Jewish hospitals sprang into existence not so much to provide religious services to Jewish patients, but to provide jobs for Jewish doctors. At the turn of the century, Jewish doctors with excellent training discovered that because of their Jewishness, they could not obtain positions on the staffs of general and sectarian hospitals. Jewish hospitals were a response to the rankest kind of anti-Semitism, as were many other institutions in Jewish life, such as some of the social welfare agencies and homes for the aged.

A fascinating study could be made some day of how Jews gradually found themselves turned away from social clubs such as the Union League Club in Philadelphia and the more prestigious city and country clubs all over the country.[14] This process ultimately led to the formation of Jewish social clubs and a growing sense of estrangement from the non-Jewish community.

One of the great dilemmas confronting the Jew today is his confusion over his relationships with non-Jews. At one and the same time he feels socially uncomfortable with non-Jews and also a need to draw closer to those non-Jews who occupy similar professional and social positions. The curtains which are open during the daytime often are drawn closed at night. There are many and notable exceptions to this pattern, of course, yet it is perceived to be a more and more persistent one at the cost of valuable communication and interchange. The demise of brotherhood week, as feeble a reed as that was, is but a further sign of the erosion of communication. For their part, Jews may be perceived as turning inward, toward their own community. Despite the presence of occasional interreligious dialogues, formal communications between Christian and Jewish laymen have been diminishing rather than growing.

Jewish life, as I have noted, manifests a tension between the secular and the religious. The question of who represents the Jewish community is more than an academic one. Is it the leadership of the secular Jewish Federation, or the agencies designed to protect Jews from anti-Semitism, such as the American Jewish Committee, the Anti-Defamation League, or the American Jewish Congress? Or is leadership to be placed in the hands of rabbis and synagogue officials? The contest is as old as the struggle between priests and prophets and there are historic parallels in the Jewish experience in Babylonia, Spain, and Eastern Europe. In a very crucial sense, the struggle is symbolic of the vitality of the Jewish community and reveals a democratic spirit in which leadership may indeed be contested.

If there is one characteristic which remains a prominent feature of the Jewish experience in America, it is the recognition of pain. Jews have come to know suffering first hand, and their encounters with persecution have led to a deep awareness of not only the anguish of their own people, but of others as well. If Jews appear to be at the vanguard of humanitarian causes, it may be because large numbers of Jews find the meaning of their religiousness in causes that promote the well-being of others. If, as Irving Howe has pointed out, blacks were the obsession of Americans, just as in Europe Jews were the obsession of Christians, then no Jew could rest comfortably with this recognition.[15] Jews were often found in leadership positions in the civil rights movement. To be sure, there were Jews who identified with oppressive forces in American society, but for vast numbers of American Jews, the cause of black emancipation took on a note of religious commitment, and even when black leaders insisted on directing their own destinies, Jewish leadership remained committed to the cause of racial equality. This is not to say that black-Jewish relationships have not been strained by historic circumstances. The rejection of white leadership, conflicts over affirmative action, and radical rhetoric have taken their toll. These together with Jewish fears of anti-Semitism and struggles over housing and jobs have not made the task of reconciliation easy. Yet the Jewish community cannot forget the pain and it seems to keep the dialogue alive.

The six million Jews in this country count for less than 3% of the population of the United Staes, yet they occupy prominent roles in the political and social structure of the country. This prominence leads itself to exaggerated charges of Jewish importance, and as a matter of fact, Jews are largely absent from the power structure as well as from the interlocking directorates of large banks and insurance companies. Yet Jews are painfully aware, as Stalin once noted, that a little bit of anti-Semitism may be a useful thing, and so their role in social and political life is tinged with more than a touch of defensiveness.

As a matter of fact, it is the struggle to normalize Jewish participation in America that has been most characteristic of the Jewish experience. To be allowed its sinners as well as its saints, to be neither unduly idolized nor villified, to be "loose" about self-hating Jewish comedians and writers, and to provide the climate where they in turn need not be self-hating, this is indeed one of the goals of the Jew in the twentieth century.

Yet, at the same time, there is something in the Jewish psyche that says, "we can never be like everyone else." The meaning of our diaspora is to remember values that others may have forgotten. Our chosenness is not for special glory, but for special service. If Israel's proclamation of the oneness of God means anything, it means that this unique dialogue cannot be ended, even in a land where perfect freedom might still be vouchsafed to every human being and a Jew could still aspire to be president of the United States.

Judaism in the United States has survived the adjustment required of a people coming to a new land. It has defended itself in the face of anti-Semitism. It has felt free to both espouse Zionism and seek an accommodation to the American way of life. The question still remains as to whether Judaism can survive success as well as persecution, freedom, and anti-Semitism. It is perhaps a miracle of faith that in spite of inducements to do otherwise, the Jewish faith and the God of Israel have maintained their compelling spirit.

My own family experience may be somewhat atypical and yet it tells a story about Jews and about a faith that would not be crushed.

My great-grandfather, Aaron Marx, came to this country in the 1840s. He was a policeman in Cleveland and he fought in the Civil War. A Policeman? He was really a truant officer, banished to this position because he was afraid to arrest anybody.

My grandfather, Joseph Marx, was a grocer. He used to get up at five o'clock in the morning to buy vegetables in the market so that he could sell them fresh from his wagon and then from a small store that he owned. One day, Joseph Marx came home and announced that he was through with Judaism; from now on he would be a Christian Scientist. He had served on a jury in Cleveland and another juror had convinced him that Christian Science would help his ailing wife.

My father is an attorney in Cleveland. Something happened to him when he was in his teens that made him decide that he could not follow his father's conversion. He determined to remain in the Jewish faith. He attended a Reform synagogue whose services were held not on a Friday night, but on Sunday morning. He was and is a deeply spiritual man and attends services every Sunday morning.

I became a rabbi. I am committed to the God of my fathers, to discovering my past. I felt the hand of God enter my life when I decided to become a rabbi and, again, to join Martin Luther King one Friday af-

91

ternoon as he sought to integrate Chicago Lawn.

In my bones, I feel the moral urgings of my German forebears. I feel the romantic impulse of the Spaniards who are part of my mother's family tradition. I also feel drawn to the ceremonial nostalgia of my Russian brothers — a nostalgia which I can only try to reconstruct but not remember. My Judaism is to be found in all of these traditions and also in something that transcends them all. I know that I am only a link in the chain which keeps my faith alive. That it has been kept alive is part of the miracle and challenge of a history and a tradition that cannot, will not die.

NOTES

1. Quoted by Zosa Szajkowski, "The Attitude of American Jews to East European Jewish Immigration (1881-1893)," Publication of the American Jewish Historical Society, Number XL, September, 1950 - June, 1951, p. 223.

2. Leon Huhner, "Asser Levy" in The Jewish Experience in America, edited by Abraham J. Karp, New York.

3. Jacob R. Marcus, Studies in American Jewish History, p. 82

4. Isaac M. Wise, Reminiscences, pp. 37-38.

5. Ibid, pp. 165-166.

6. Ibid, pp. 210-211.

7. Irving Howe, World of Our Fathers, pp. 160-161.

8. Oscar Handlin, The Uprooted, p. 79.

9. Hannah Arendt, Origins of Totalitarianism, Part One, p. 87.

10. 1 Samuel 8: 11-12.

11. Howe, op. cit., p. 195.

12. Nathan Glazer, American Judaism, pp. 85 ff.

13. Yearbook of the Central Conference of American Rabbis, Vol. I, pp. 120-123, (Pittsburgh Platform)

14. E. Digby Baltzell, The Protestant Establishment, pp. 374-79.

15. Howe, op. cit., p. 631.

BIBLIOGRAPHY

Arendt, Hannah, The Origins of Totalitarianism (New York: Meridian Books, 1958).

Baltzell, E. Digby, The Protestant Establishment, (New York: Random, 1964).

Glazer, Nathan, American Judaism (Chicago: University of Chicago Press, 1957).

Handlin, Oscar, The Uprooted (Boston: Little, Brown, 1951).

Howe, Irving, World of Our Fathers (New York: Harcourt Brace, 1976).

The Jewish Experience in America, edited by Abraham J. Karp, (New York: KTAV, 1969).

The Jews of the United States, 1790-1840, A Documentary History, edited by Joseph L. Blau and Salo W. Baron, (New York: Columbia University Press, 1963).

Marcus, Jacob Rader, Studies in American Jewish History (Cincinnati: KTAV, 1969).

Modern Jewish History, edited by Robert Chazan and Marc Lee Raphael, (New York : Schocken, 1974).

Wise, Isaac M., Reminiscences (Cincinnati, 1901).

CATHOLICISM IN AMERICA: THE SEARCH FOR UNITY AND ACCEPTABILITY

By JOHN T. PAWLIKOWSKI, OSM

Non-Catholic Americans have traditionally looked upon the Catholic Church as a rigid, monolithic institution. Since the II Vatican Council, much of that image has been shattered. What perhaps is not yet sufficiently realized by non-Catholics is that underneath the somewhat real, somewhat imagined notion of conformity there always existed tremendous diversity and pluralism within American Catholicism. Looking back over the history of the Catholic presence in the United States, one can legitimately describe it from one perspective as a struggle for unity and from another as a search for acceptability.

The earliest parents of American Catholicism were Spanish and French. They were colonists and missionaries. They knew all the devotion of the missionaries and all the indifference of the colonists. In the English territories, on the other hand, the first Catholics were a persecuted minority, a band of refugees. Catholics were oppressed in the Puritan domains of New England and in the Anglican domains of Virginia. In the territory of Maryland, founded by the Catholic Lord Baltimore, and in the open atmosphere of Quaker Pennsylvania a refugee situation prevailed. The colony of Maryland, the first establishment of Catholics under the protection of the English Crown, was not founded until 1629. The first French priests, on the contrary, arrived in 1614. And the Spanish mission, by far the most ancient of all, dates from 1540 in New Mexico and from 1577 in Florida.

Catholic America is increasingly conscious that its Spanish element constitutes one of its most authentic roots. Nearly a quarter of contemporary American Catholics are Spanish-speaking. Yet this brand of the Catholic spirit has existed somewhat unnoticed in mainstream American Catholicism with little or no influence upon national institutions. The present emergence of Spanish-speaking Catholics into the center of their church's life in the United States may provide one of the most significant modifications in American Catholicism's future structures and spirit. It

93

likely will produce a greater concern for social justice, as already has been evidenced in the strong support given the Farmworkers struggle and the Farah Pants unionization efforts by the national Catholic hierarchy — the most solid pro-justice stand it has taken outside of the abortion issue. It may also turn American Catholicism away from its strongly European orientation toward a greater concern for Latin America. This could well have an effect on the Catholic church's view of American foreign policy. The newly aroused Spanish-speaking element in the church prevailed upon the American Bishops last fall to encourage the study of the theology of liberation in all American Catholic seminaries. But this Spanish-speaking element may also promote a somewhat more traditional emphasis in the areas of doctrine, liturgy and ecumenical relations.

Fr. George Tavard makes a telling point about the nature of early American Catholicism. "The prehistory of Catholicism in the United States does not coincide with that of American Catholicism. Catholicism was established in the West before it began in the East. The history of the United States goes in the opposite direction" (*Catholicism, USA*, p. 12). After the War of Independence parts of New France and New Spain were taken over by the English colonies, both politically and culturally. The Catholics in these two regions found themselves immersed in the world of American pioneers who regarded them as an element with a foreign language and a different religion. From a dominant class, Catholics quickly assumed the role of a definite minority. In some ways we can date American Catholicism from the moment that the Catholic renaissance in the Eastern part of the country, marked by the arrival of waves of Catholic immigrants and the multiplication of English-speaking bishoprics, took charge of these "new" territories. This rapid societal transformation of American Catholicism brought with it the struggle for acceptability in what was now a basically Protestant America.

On the one hand, a strong trend to prove that Catholics were truly Americans emerged. Surnames were changed in many cases and the American flag began to appear in church sanctuaries. The triumph of the English-speaking element in the Roman church also gave the Irish in particular the ability to begin to dominate the institutional side of American Catholicism. The Spanish component, though numerically strong, became a somewhat invisible minority within a minority.

Alongside the drive for acceptability the desire for preservation of the Catholic identity, in some cases the Catholic ethnic identity, remained strong. Catholics began an extensive school system of their own, not because they were necessarily opposed to secular education as such, but because the so-called "public school" was in many cases very Protestant orientated. Many of the immigrants from Southern and Eastern Europe tried to preserve some of their particular Catholic traditions over against the dominant Northern European ethos of both the United States and the national Catholic church. This led to the establishment of a network of so-called "national" parishes within most dioceses to accommodate non-English-speaking people. In some places such as Chicago virtual "sub-dioceses" for certain ethnic groups like the Poles developed. Thus, as George Tavard has accurately pointed out, "one of the most noticeable characteristics of 19th century America is precisely the growth of national groups among the Catholics" (*Ibid.* p. 31).

During the nineteenth century the homogeneity which had existed in the earlier days of American Catholicism tended at first to yield to a variegated mosaic of "particular" catholicisms. The principle of unity rooted in acceptance of the American society and the belief that most immigrants would eventually accept its democratic ideals. However, their first goal remained the maintenance of their European cultural identity. The problem was complicated by the somewhat spontaneous identification of the Irish group with American Catholicism. The serious problem of nationalities reaffirmed itself with each new immigrant group, with traces of this continuing today. The new ethnic awareness that dominates some sectors of present-day society in the Unites States has resurrected some of these tensions especially among the Slavs and Italians.

The problem of assimilating immigrants was still more traumatic when Eastern-rite Catholics arrived on the scene. For Catholics of the Latin-rite, the question was basically a matter of assuring them religious instruction in their native language for a generation or two until such time as it was possible for the people to adequately handle the English language. The situation, however, was quite different for Eastern-rite Catholics. The latter came relatively late, around the 1880s. But the Latin clergy did not take any notice of what was happening. Not satisfied with wanting to Americanize the new arrivals, they tried to Latinize them as well. Catholics of the Byzantine or Armenian rites, sometimes led by married clergy, were often treated as heretical groups by the Latin-rite clergy. It took until 1907 for the situation of the Eastern Catholics to be clarified by the formation of a Ukrainian exarchate for the United States with its center in Philadelphia. A number of other separate dioceses for Ukrainians, Ruthenians, Melkites and Maronites have been created since then. But in many ways the psychology of American Catholicism still places the Eastern-rite Catholics on the extreme outer fringes of American Catholicism. Most non-Catholics and Latin-rite Catholics are totally unaware that two Catholic dioceses exist in Chicago, not simply the one presided over by Cardinal Cody.

It is important to recognize that there was no *a priori* reason why American Catholicism should be Latin rather than Byzantine. Due to the dimensions of the Irish immigration and to the actions of the great bishops of the nineteenth century, Irish Catholics gradually dominated, with Germans, Poles, Italians, Spaniards and Canadians forming minorities. After passing through a phase of linguistic pluralism, American Catholicism became English-speaking, with German, Polish, Italian, Spanish and French as more or less important second languages. This process had the effect of uniting everyone culturally in the English language and in the American way of life. No one seriously contemplated a plurality of rites as an answer to the immigration waves, a plurality that would have left American Catholicism something less than exclusively Latin. The plurality-conformity dialectic, which strongly surfaced in the bishopric of the great John England, eventually weighed heavily on the side of conformism.

One interesting example of the internal dominance of the Northern European style of Catholicism in the United States emerges from the classic St. Louis University studies on the image of racial and religious outgroups in Catholic teaching materials (see my *Catechetics and Prejudice*). While these studies primarily surfaced the image of non-Catholics and non-whites in the Catholic curriculum, they also showed that even Catholics who did not fit into the Northern European pattern were by inference considered outsiders. Thus those Southern and East European Catholics who were part of the second great wave of immigration together with Spanish-speaking and black Catholics definitely appear as outgroups in the religion, literature and social studies texts supposedly designed for use by *all* American Catholics. The ethos and spirit of the Catholicism portrayed in these textbooks was decidedly shaped by the Northern European cultural mold. Here is another illustration of the drive for conformism.

The problem of external conformism, i.e. becoming accepted by the Protestant American majority, produced two other trends within American Catholicism that are worthy of note. The first one was marked by hostility towards the Protestant establishment. This attitude is termed by Tavard "vengeful Catholicism" (*Catholicism, USA*, p. 36). In large part it grew up in response to sensational literature coupled with anti-Catholic attacks. The Provincial Council of Baltimore of 1833 noted the progress of aggressive anti-Catholicism among some Americans. Works appeared treating pornographic themes in convent settings. Samuel Morse's *Foreign Conspiracy Against the Liberties of the U.S.* (1834) opened a long list of pretended studies on the political dealings of the Catholic Church. Several publications led to anti-Catholic riots and burnings. At the height of the anti-Catholic crisis, the Council of Baltimore of 1843 showed wisdom when it urged the Catholic population to strengthen its social bonds with their non-Catholic neighbors. The hierarchy appeared to want to overlook the outrages against Catholics. But the desires of bishops are not the only elements that influence sociological reality. The hotheads who were "out to get the Catholics" in 1835 assured the birth within American Catholicism of one of its least Catholic phenomena, the facility with which it believes itself abused for the faith.

The ecumenical atmosphere following the II Vatican Council has done much to erase this "under attack" feeling from the United States Catholic psyche. But recently the school aid question and the abortion issue have brought it to the surface again in sections of the Catholic church. Fr. Andrew Greeley has taken this as one of his favorite themes of late. And Cardinal Kroll of Philadelphia, former head of the American Bishops, has raised it in a number of public speeches. The emphasis now, however, is not so outrightly anti-Protestant as it is anti-liberal Protestant/Jewish. And Fr. Virgil Blum has been working on organizing a kind of Catholic equivalent of the Jewish Anti-Defamation League. It is still too early to tell whether this trend will generate widespread support among rank-and-file Catholics or whether it will quietly fade away after an initial big splash.

The second trend produced by the "external conformism" problem has led in a much more positive and constructive direction. It has had several phases, but I will confine myself to only two of them in this short presentation.

The general progress of American Catholics by the end of the nineteenth century led to a favorable impression of its patterns among some European Catholics, particularly in France. Foreign observers overlooked the absence of Catholics from key positions of leadership and influence in this country. Instead they were impressed by the numerical growth, increasing prosperity and complete freedom which Catholics enjoyed in America. To many French Catholics, especially harassed by the anti-clerical laws of the Third Republic, the American Church appeared a worthy object for emulation. But powerful conservative forces within the French Church frowned upon what they regarded as the American departure from traditional Catholic mores. They saw, for example, in the great Fr. Isaac Hecker's emphasis on partial agreements rather than disagreement with Protestants a watering down of Catholic doctrine. Some Catholics in the United States felt that such actions as the participation of Catholic church people in the World Parliament of Religions at the Chicago World's Fair of 1893, the open approach of bishops like Gibbons, Ireland and Keane to the problem of secret societies, and the efforts of Archbishop Ireland to find a compromise between the public and parochial schools fostered liberal tendencies which would imperil the integrity of the Catholic faith. At the head of these concerned American Catholics stood Archbishop Corrigan of New York who found support from fellow members of the hierarchy, particularly among those of German descent.

As a result of these differences, what Bishop Keane characterized as "the war of ideas" grew more intense. A careless French translation of Walter Elliot's *Life of Father Hecker* in 1897 sparked an angry outburst that filled the columns of Catholic journals on both sides of the Atlantic for several years. The controversy over what was termed the Americanist heresy became so heated that a commission of cardinals was eventually appointed by Pope Leo XIII to study the entire situation. The commission's findings resulted in the papal letter *Testem benevolentiae* of January 22, 1899, addressed to Cardinal Gibbons wherein the Pope summarized certain false doctrines which, as he was careful to say, were imputed to some within the American Church. With the publication of this papal letter each side believed that it had been vindicated. More conservative prelates like those of the provinces of New York and Milwaukee thanked the Holy Father for saving the American Church from the danger of heresy, while Cardinal Gibbons made it clear to Leo XIII that none of the views he condemned were in fact being held by people in the American church, expressing indignation that "Americanism" was the word used to describe such views.

The "Americanist heresy" controversy is significant because it brought to the fore the running battle within the church about the adaptation of Catholicism to a social-cultural milieu that was different from that found in Europe. Specifically those accused of being Americanist heretics were people who felt that the atmosphere of religious pluralism that generally characterized the American social fabric had to exercise an influence on the shape and style of Catholic expression in America. This spirit within the American Catholic church did not die with the publication of *Testem benevolentiae.* Rather it continued to grow and develop, eventually manifesting itself in the second of the constructive trends emerging from the struggle for external conformism.

This second trend was the development of a theology of religious liberty. The undoubted leader in this area was the late John Courtney Murray, SJ. Through his writings and those of others the experience of American Catholicism in a situation where at least religious toleration if not complete harmony was the rule rather than the exception came to modify the church's basic ecclesiology. The culmination of this movement occurred in the decree of the II Vatican Council on Religious Liberty and on the Church's Relationship to the Jewish People. Both these documents reflect a uniquely American spirit and stand as the most distinctive contribution by the American church to the Council. Without the full and active support of the American bishops neither of these documents could have passed the Council.

At this point it would be useful to move away somewhat from the unity/acceptability theme to highlight several other prominent features of American Catholic life that have influenced its piety and practicality. High on any list of fundamental characteristics of American Catholicism must be what the dean of historians of Catholic America, John Tracy Ellis, has termed its "anti-intellectualism". This was evident to some leaders who attempted to undergird American Catholic piety with a sound intellectual foundation. Due largely to the persistence, intelligence and resourcefulness of Bishop Spaulding the Catholic University of America opened at Washington in 1889 and became in the years that followed the center of much that was best in Catholic thought and scholarship. In that major undertaking the Bishop of Peoria had the warm support of men like Gibbons, Keane and Ireland, once they became convinced that such an educational institution was a viable possibility. Archbishop Ireland needed little urging, for as he said in his sermon at the centennial of the American hierarchy a few days before the university opened: "This is an intellectual age...Catholics must excel in religious knowledge.... They must be in the foreground of intellectual movements of all kinds. The age will not take kindly to religious knowledge separated from secular knowledge."

As the century drew to a close, these bishops continued to do all within their power to heighten the intellectual tone of Catholic life. But their goals were never fully realized. As John Tracy Ellis has bluntly put it, "The failure of American Catholics to achieve distinction in the world of scholarship and learning still remains the most striking weakness of what is otherwise perhaps the strongest branch of the universal Church" (*American Catholicism*, p. 119). No well-informed Catholic can severely quarrel with a similar judgment expressed by Professor D. W. Brogan of Cambridge University, "In no Western society is the intellectual prestige of Catholics lower than in that country where, in such respects as wealth, members and strength of organization, it is so powerful" (quoted in *American Catholicism*, p. 119).

George Tavard attributes the anti-intellectual tradition in American Catholicism in part to the emphasis on Canon Law in the American church which began with Bishop John England and the twelve Councils of Baltimore as a means of securing unity in the church. In America there arose the most extensive body of canonical regulations fashioned in modern times by the hierarchy of a single country. On the other hand, the American clergy have given few theologians to the church. Through the stress on canonical legislation American Catholic life in the nineteenth century counterbalanced its pluralism of origin by a psychological and social conformism, and the clergy were trained with a view to a well-ordered administration rather than with a view to extensive theological knowledge. To this day, there still is no widely respected doctoral degree in theology offered by any Catholic university in this country. The vast majority of American Catholics study theology on a doctoral level overseas or increasingly in schools such as the University of Chicago's Divinity School where in a few short years Catholics have become the largest single denominational bloc.

Another important component of American Catholicism has been its involvement in social issues. This may sound somewhat surprising to those not well acquainted with the development of the American church. Certainly this is not the best known public trait of the Catholic Church in this land. American Catholicism has never produced the social theorists or theologians that Protestantism has. There are no Niebuhrs, Parsons, Rauschenbusches or the like. But as James Hastings Nichols, no special friend of Roman Catholicism, has indicated, in many ways it represents the best social action doctrine of any church in America. Andrew Greeley has shown how this social action doctrine "would inspire hundreds and perhaps even thousands of young Catholic progressive reformers, liberals and even radicals in the first half of the twentieth century. It would have no difficulty reconciling itself with some elements in the mainstream of American social reform. Its thought and action would represent one of the happier marriages between the Catholic Church and American society" (*The Catholic Experience*, p. 217). Its names included John Ryan and Dorothy Day, the "Chicago Group" of Reynold Hillenbrand, Daniel Cantwell, John Egan and others, as well as labor reformers such as Terence Powderly, first Grand Master Workman of the Knights of Labor, and "Black John" Mitchell, President of the United Mine Workers of America. It was in the improvement of the conditions of the American worker that Catholic social action had its greatest impact on American society. From the time that Cardinal Gibbons took his strong stand in favor of the Knights of Labor, the church was publicly indentified with the interests of the working class. As a result the American Catholic working class has never been alientated from the church in the manner that has taken place in Europe. Labor historians have shown that Catholic influence helped to account for the moderate social philosophy and policies of the American Federation of Labor and for the absence of a political labor party in the United States.

Unfortunately, as Fr. Greeley has himself noted, the highly successful American Catholic social doctrines attracted relatively little grass-roots support, exercised only minimal influence on Catholic education, and at no time could command widespread enthusiasm in the Catholic press. "The failure of the American Church," he says, "to make more than it did out of its quite impressive social reform tradition must be evaluated as a major failure of the Americanizing element in the history of the Catholic Church in the United States" (*Ibid.*, p. 246). The failure of this social action doctrine to take hold of the masses is best revealed in the widespread support given to the famous radio-priest Charles E. Coughlin with his vitriolic outbursts against Jews and the New Deal.

One area of social concern where the record of the American Catholic Church is not good is that of racism. The historian Sydney Ahlstrom has noted that anti-Catholic attitudes of most participants in the anti-slavery movement were steadily heightened because the Roman Catholic hierarchy remained noncommitted on slavery and almost completely unrepresented in the abolitionist crusade. The official Catholic position was that slavery as a principle of social organization was not in itself sinful, though in 1839 Pope Gregory XVI had reiterated the church's condemnation of the slave trade. The leading American theologian of the period, Bishop Kenrick of St. Louis said, "Since such is the state of things (slavery being the status quo) nothing should be attempted against the laws nor anything be done or said that would make them bear their yoke unwillingly" (quoted in "Catholic America", *St. Anthony Messenger*, January 1976, p. 16). His teaching in the eyes of Ahlstrom shows a persistent failure to clarify the differences between the actual American form of slavery and that which the church had condoned. Thus he has been accused of equivocating.

After the Civil War, the Second Plenary Council of Baltimore (1886) came to grips with the problem of four million newly emancipated slaves. Bishop Martin Spalding, serving as apostolic delegate, took a deep interest in the black apostolate, suggesting that special prefects apostolic be appointed for the blacks. His proposal was not adopted, but nine decrees were passed to implement the ministry to blacks. The question of segregated parishes, however, was left to be decided by individual bishops according to local custom. But almost nothing came of the legislation because of the hostility of both clergy and laity toward blacks. Southern bishops appealed for workers and funds but had little success. Most religious orders, with a few notable exceptions such as the Josephites, shied away from the task for fear of alienating white patronage. Thus the noble legislation of the council was never carried out.

A major Catholic breakthrough on the racial front had to wait until 1947 when Cardinal Ritter of St. Louis ended segregation in Catholic schools, followed in 1948 by Archbishop Patrick O'Boyle of Washington. At this time there also developed in several areas of the country Catholic Interracial Councils inspired by the thought of people like Fr. John LaFarge. These local councils eventually coalesced into an umbrella national organization called the National Catholic Conference for Interracial Justice headquartered in Chicago. It was quite active in the organization of events such as the famous March on Washington. While still in existence in Washington, the organization has suffered tremendous attrition in support. In part the slack has been taken up by the National Office of Black Catholics in Washington.

There are many who feel that the black Catholic population (presently about four percent of American blacks are Catholic) will slowly die away except for the New Orleans region. Many of those currently struggling to preserve the Catholic schools in the inner city see it as the last possible attempt to maintain and increase a black presence in the American Catholic Church. But the success of their efforts is problematical at best.

As a general observation, we can say that present-day social action in American Catholicism is very much in a quandry. Many who were in the forefront of civil rights, inner city and peace work in the sixties have left the church. The bishops have taken strong stands in behalf of the Farm Workers and on the abortion issue. The bishops' program for the bicentennial titled *Liberty and Justice for All* has a decidedly social justice orientation. And a coalition of Southern bishops has issued a strong Pastoral Letter defending the rights of the people of Appalachia. But the general Catholic population, now increasingly suburban and middle class, has grown even more conservative on social questions. Some are trying to regroup and regain the momentum of the sixties by developing Justice and Peace Centers and organizations such as the John Egan Catholic Committee on Urban Ministry. While there are bright spots, the immediate prospect for the development of a strong social consciousness within a large segment of American Catholicism is not terribly promising.

In closing this brief overview of Catholicism in the United States it would be fair to assert that the problem of acceptability has been largely solved, solved too well in the eyes of some within the church. It may be that American Catholics are now too comfortably a part of mainstream America. Some are now beginning to speak of the need for American Catholics to emphasize their distinctiveness. The search for unity, however, remains as great a struggle as ever. Some of the issues are new, brought about by the sweeping reforms introduced by II Vatican. There is also a new freedom component in the church. Catholics no longer feel the same need for strict adherence to so-called official ecclesiastical positions. Regular Sunday Mass attendance has fallen off sharply and so has participation in the sacrament of Penance. Young people have become alienated by droves and in most of the large urban "Catholic" universities only a minority of students could be realistically termed fully practicing Catholics. Perhaps this is only a momentary alienation by a first generation of college educated young people from traditional Catholic homes. Yet it definitely seems to point to a significant decrease in the number of Catholics in America during the coming decades.

Last December I was interviewed by *Chicago Magazine* for my impressions on what the Catholic Church would look like in 2001. I said then and I repeat now, it is virtually impossible to answer that question. But I do feel that the following factors among others will influence the contour of the church at the turn of the century: (1) the direction the Spanish-speaking element in the church takes; (2) whether black Catholics will develop strength; (3) whether the current charismatic push will reinforce the traditional anti-intellectualism of American Catholicism; (4) whether some of the currently alienated Catholic young people will regain a sense of identity within the framework of the church; (5) whether Catholic leadership, both in this country and in Rome develops a more open style; and (6) what role women will come to play in church leadership. My suspicion is, however, that no matter what precise direction the American church takes the year 2001 will still find it struggling for internal unity. That after all, as we have seen above, has been one of its principal features and one might assert one of its chief strengths since its inception in the colonial era.

SUGGESTED BIBLIOGRAPHY

1. John Cogley, *Catholic America*. Doubleday, paperback.

   A generally thematic interpretation of the Catholic experience in the United States by one of its original outstanding lay leaders who has now become a member of the Episcopal Church.

2. John Tracy Ellis, *American Catholicism*. Second Edition, Revised. University of Chicago Press, paperback.

   The single most important interpretation of the American Catholic Church by the Dean of Catholic Church historians in the United States. The book follows the development of Catholicism in this country chronologically.

3. Andrew M. Greeley, *The Catholic Experience: An Interpretation of the History of American Catholicism*. (Doubleday & Co.) No paperback edition available.

   An interpretation of American Catholicism through a detailed focus on some of its great figures and movements. It contains the famous chapter on John Kennedy, Doctor of Church.

4. David J. O'Brien, *The Renewal of American Catholicism*. Paulist-Newman paperback.

   A thematic interpretation of American Catholicism by another major name in Catholic historical circles.

5. John T. Pawlikowski. *Catechetics and Prejudice*. Paulist Press, paperback.

   A summary and analysis of the classic St. Louis University studies on how Catholic educational materials view racial and religious outgroups. Also valuable for perspective on how Catholics viewed themselves in these materials.

6. George H. Tavard. *Catholicism USA*. Newman Press. No paperback edition available.

   A concise chronological account of American Catholicism with interpretation interspersed.

THEOLOGY AND SOCIAL ACTIVISM

By VICTOR OBENHAUS

The original title assigned for this presentation was "The Social Gospel and Activism." I took the liberty of suggesting the change. The Social Gospel is not a theology in the sense that Karl Barth's thought constitutes a theology, or in the sense of any other theologian whose thought has resulted in a system. It is significant, however, that the most satisfying and comprehensive interpreter of the Social Gospel, Walter Rauschenbusch, produced *A Theology for the Social Gospel* for the Taylor Lectures at Yale in 1917. These lectures constituted his last book. He died the following year.

Rauschenbusch knew that the Social Gospel had to be undergirded by a theology, a theology that was primarily a way of understanding Jesus' total message, his thought, his words to his own period, his life as he lived it. These elements were fused into a total pattern of life for his followers. That configuration gripped the imaginations of many men and women to create the "Social Gospel." These individuals and their successors worked diligently at the process of developing theological foundations for responsible living based on their Christian heritage. One has only to review the recent Hartford Declaration and the Boston Affirmation to realize that the issues with which Washington Gladden, Walter Rauschenbusch, Richard Ely, Graham Taylor, and a host of others wrestled constitute a highly current theme.

Henry P. Van Dusen called the Social Gospel "America's greatest contribution to religion." Reinhold Niebuhr, shortly before his death, when asked what he might do differently if he could live his life again, replied that he would give more attention to the Social Gospel. He himself was a product in large measure of that gospel, having read much of Rauschenbusch in his early ministry. Niebuhr is author of the statement that Rauschenbusch was "the real founder of social Christianity in this country and its most brilliant and generally satisfying exponent."[1]

Since the lives and writings of the Social Gospel pioneers have been fully documented elsewhere, amplification of such material in any detail here is unnecessary. Suffice it to say that Chicago Theological Seminary along with every "liberal" seminary in this country has been the beneficiary of the Social Gospel's impact and has been in a large measure shaped by it. In addition to CTS that would include Harvard, Andover Newton, Yale, Boston, Union, though later heavily tinged with neo-orthodoxy, Colgate Rochester, Oberlin, now merged with Vanderbilt, Chicago's Divinity School, McCormick, Garrett, Iliff, Pacific School of Theology, Southern California School of Religion, and more recently Christian Theological Seminary in Indianapolis. These are seminaries which did not capitulate in any great degree to the wave of neo-orthodoxy which swept the country following World War II.

CLIMATE PRODUCING THE SOCIAL GOSPEL

No single definition or fully satisfying statement describes the Social Gospel. It was the product of an era in American history. It emerged at a time when the physical sciences were burgeoning. Darwin and his *Origin of the Species* jarred many religious presuppositions. The science of economics was in its infancy. Richard T. Ely, said to be the layman who had greater influence on the economic thought of the clergy than any other individual, founded the American Economics Association at Johns Hopkins. He later moved to the University of Wisconsin. Ely was a thoroughly dedicated Christian who related economics to the Bible as no one had ever done before. He opened the whole area of economics for study in seminaries and by ministers and fellow laymen. Sociology was in its infancy. The first head of the Sociology Department at the University of Chicago was a clergyman. The first chaplain of the University was a sociologist (Charles R. Henderson). Graham Taylor was called to Chicago Theological Seminary as the first Professor of Christian Sociology in the nation. Inseparable from the discipline of sociology is the function of research. Under the impetus of the Social Gospel, the study of religious institutions, notably the church, both rural and urban, emerged. CTS played an important part in religious research.

Most important in the development of the Social Gospel was the plethora of new discoveries leading to and stemming from biblical studies. "Higher Criticism," originating primarily among German biblical scholars, opened up a new approach to the Bible. It led to a conviction that Jesus' message was influenced by the times and circumstances in which he lived. Scholars felt that Jesus, a very human figure as well as divine, would have more meaning for individuals in the contemporary period if they could understand what he really meant. Harnack in Germany was a leading exponent of this approach to the Bible. Rauschenbusch and large numbers of other American clergymen studied with him. A number of German universities drew American theologians seeking the new and radical interpretation of Scripture. The Bible took on new meaning. It dealt not only with the esoteric things of the spirit, but was filled with specific injunctions for individual and societal conduct. William Rainey Harper, the guiding genius of the new University of Chicago and its first president, had hundreds of pastors studying Hebrew in correspondence courses so that they could understand the Prophets. The Divinity School of the University of Chicago may well have been the first divinity school emerging from the Social Gospel Movement. And incongruous as it may seem, Harper, the president of a burgeoning new first rate university, took time to serve as the superintendent of the Sunday School of the nearby Hyde Park Baptist Church (1897-1905); he wanted to have this process of education for understanding the message of the Prophets and Jesus begin at the earliest possible age. Understandably, the Religious Education Association had its beginnings in this biblical, educational, theologically innovative milieu in 1903.

SOME MAJOR EMPHASES

However, more than the increased appropriation of scientific study and its use in technology, more than the new disciplines of psychology and sociology, more than the new biblical discoveries, is required to understand the large scale involvement of laymen and clergy to modify the social ills exacerbated by the new industrialism. As new developments in science made possible phenomenal growth in manufacturing, transportation, communication so did new biblical studies sensitize individuals to the demands of historic faith upon them to modify the rapacities and injustices of the fast industrial emergence.

Walter Rauschenbusch's experience with sweatshops and misery as a pastor in Hell's Kitchen in New York convinced him of the necessity for labor organizations. The Social Gospel Movement gave rise to extensive support of the Labor Movement, both in denominational affirmations and institutional form, such as the Labor Temple of the Presbyterians. A further expression took the form of the Religion and Labor Foundation, made up largely of clergy and religiously disposed labor leadership. There was even a seminary division with a full-time executive which was still in existence when I came to CTS. Every major figure in the Social Gospel Movement was a staunch supporter of the Labor Movement.

The Cooperative Movement began in Rochdale, England in 1848 and went into full swing during the period of the Social Gospel's greatest strength. It became one of the focal points of Social Gospel action. Many ministers became full-time workers in the Cooperative Movement because it gave promise of being the means by which the Gospel could be expressed in the economic sphere. Many lay workers, too, felt this was a way in which their Christian witness could be made in the so-called secular world. It is an interesting phenomenon that the one who possibly did more to stimulate the conviction that the Cooperative Movement was

Christian faith in action was the frail but dynamic little man from Osaka and Kobe, Toyohika Kagawa. He drew immense crowds in the United States when he preached the message of cooperatives as the Christian way in economics. In 1957 enough people were still imbued with this conviction that the National Council of Churches held a national conference on the religious significance of the Cooperative Movement.

The period of the Social Gospel's greatest strength is the period in which the urban problem came to the fore. Curiously, however, religious research did not begin with the cities. The plight of the deteriorating rural communities first caught the attention of the students of American society. People were leaving the countryside for the cities. Farms were getting bigger and families smaller. Country churches were dying at the rate of 400 a year. The mutual dependence of the urban churches upon the rural churches began to become apparent. With the disappearance of the rural churches would come the decay of urban religion. Partly to stem this tide the Country Life Movement under Gifford Pinchot and Theodore Roosevelt came into being backed by the studies of Charles Galpin of the University of Wisconsin and an enthusiastic new group of rural sociologists. Every major denomination, and some not so major, developed Town and Country Departments. Many seminaries had departments and professorships related to town and country churches.

As religious life in the cities presented new problems, interest logically turned to the study of the welfare of the urban churches. The Institute for Social and Religious Research located at Columbia University undertook the gargantuan task of attempting to survey the religious situation in every county in the United States. A Rockefeller grant ran out before completion of the study, but it was a landmark in religious research. Its director was Harlan Paul Douglass, the foremost figure in religious research in his day. Symbolically Douglass turned his own interest from the rural to the urban church. Most denominations have also turned their attention from the rural to the urban scene. Suffice it to say that the religious research movement which is still part of the religious scene was an outgrowth of the Social Gospel.

No discussion of the relation between religion and the city would be complete without mentioning the Settlement House Movement. Waves of immigration literally dumped millions of strangers into our cities. Unfamiliar with the customs and language of the new land, they were exploited in their work and by the people who provided them places to live. Such inhumanity touched some church people, and the Settlement House Movement was a manifestation of their concern. Britain's Toynbee Hall served as a model for expressions of American intentions. Language instruction became the major aspect of the movement in this country. True to the Scriptures, here was a stranger in our gates who needed protection.

Not all settlement houses were religiously affiliated, but almost all of them had basic religious motivation and a large number were denominationaliy affiliated. The Chicago Commons is a good illustration. When Graham Taylor was brought from Hartford to CTS, he accepted on the condition that he might hold his classes and live in an immigrant area. He established Chicago Commons where he lived with his family on the near northwest side. It became his seminary classroom as well as a center for bringing aid to the area and the city at large. With his contemporary, Jane Addams at Hull House, he worked at the problems of poverty, disease and tragedy which he found in the booming city with all of its attendant corruption. With his unusual vision he set out to establish the Chicago School of Philanthropy, which later became the School of Social Service Administration of the University of Chicago.

Leaders of the Social Gospel were interested in denominations primarily for their capacity to effect change in society. Their interest in ecumenism was largely due to its potential for social usefulness. The Faith and Order Movement of the World Council of Churches had been meeting for many years around common elements of faith and points of divergence. Its leadership realized that a functional basis could be found in common activities. Meanwhile the Life and Work Movement, which had been meeting for years also, was coming to realize that it needed a more solid theological base than the Social Gospel proponents had provided. This fact became evident in the simultaneous sessions of the two groups, the former held at Edinburgh and the latter at Oxford during 1937 just as the Hitler terror was beginning to emerge in Europe. The Oxford Conference and its successors, the Amsterdam and Evanston Conferences, still reflect a measure of the Social Gospel's influence.

FAITH, PERSONS AND ACTION

Citing the cultural phenomena which gave rise to the movement and the measures developed as responses does not explain rationale and motivation. What was the theological undergirding which produced so great a measure of activity? The European designation of American accomplishments was "activismus." There was no European counterpart. Many assumed that American expressions growing out of the biblical mandates were basically shallow. There was no full orbed theological framework. But there were attempts to provide structure for the movement.

Earliest of the truly major figures of the Social Gospel was Washington Gladden (1836-1918), in one sense its real pioneer.[2] In addition to pastorates in Springfield, Massachusetts, and the First Congregational Church of Columbus, Ohio, (1882-1918), he was religious editor of the *Independent*, a progressive journal flourishing in the late nineteenth century, greatly in demand as a lecturer and writer. He was a man of broad scholarship, great personal piety and social convictions and persuasiveness. He incorporated in his writing and preaching many of the same emphases later lifted up by Rauschenbusch. He, too, found the new approach to the Bible liberating. He espoused the concept of the Brotherhood of Man with its expectation that it could lead toward man's perfection. He found the idea of the Kingdom, so dominant in Jesus' thought to be highly realistic, ultimately coming to the glorious fulfillment in the Law of Love recognized as the Law of Life. Gladden gave much attention to the struggle between classes and focused strongly on the Labor Movement as a means of achieving egalitarianism. Perhaps because of the period in which he was nurtured, he had a greater confidence in America's fulfillment of its role as exemplar of what a Christian nation might be. The church could be the instrument by which America might perform that function. Gladden's idealism has never wholly disappeared from the thought of many Christian Americans.

More significant than Gladden's time-bound political and patriotic convictions is his Christology. He wrote, "The doctrine of the person of Christ is one of the chief battlegrounds of theology." He acknowledged great indebtedness to Albert Ritschl who represented for him the modern way of thinking about Jesus Christ. Gladden quotes William Adams Brown as providing the gist of Ritschl's theology: "The true task of the theologian is to study the human Jesus, that he may learn from an analysis of his life and work what are the features of his character and ministry which gave him his unique power to uplift and transform human life." Then Gladden goes on to say, "Thus we have learned what to think about Jesus Christ, not by questioning the philosophers and dogmatists but by going first directly to him and by opening our lives to the grace which bringeth salvation and believing what he tells us about the fatherhood of God . . . This is the substance of what I believe about Jesus Christ. I do not know that I care to put any label on my belief. I would rather that it should stand on its own logic and shine by its own light." As was true for the Social Gospel as a whole, the newly discovered humanity of Jesus provided the model for all humanity.

Though Washington Gladden is considered the "Father of the Social Gospel," the great figure in giving the movement systematization and theological base was Walter Rauschenbusch. His Fellowship of the Kingdom provided something for thousands of people. For him Jesus' concept of the Kingdom of God was the center of the gospel. He wrote, "If theology is to offer an adequate doctrinal basis for the Social Gospel it must not only make room for the doctrine of the Kingdom of God but give it a central place and revise all other doctrines so that they will articulate organically with it." He noted that only two of Jesus' reported sayings contain the word 'church' . . . The church, he said is a fellowship for worship. The Kingdom is a fellowship of righteousness.[3]

The pioneer figures of the Social Gospel were not theologians in the formal sense of that word, but they were not theologically uninformed. One biographer of Rauschenbusch contends that his first interest was in salvation. He deplored the individual otherworldliness and self-centered pietism which was compounded with secular optimism and an unthinking patriotism. His confrontation with poverty opened his eyes to a new understanding of salvation. In this context the world does set the agenda for the church. The recent Hartford and Boston Affirmations may be repeating the earlier confrontations. Rauschenbusch's concept of the Kingdom implies both the immanence and the transcendence of God and man's total responsibility to God, with no bifurcation of the personal and social. Rauschenbusch believed original sin was a reality to be reckoned with. Elimination of poverty was not enough. Regeneration was the most important fact in human history. The social order could not be saved without regenerate individuals. While many analyses of the Social Gospel reveal shortcomings, especially some superficiality in the diagnosis of the human situation, its principal interpreter and protagonist cannot be labelled superficial.

Rauschenbusch was not a handwringer. He believed something could be done. He pressed for reforms in the organization of labor, income and inheritance taxes, community sponsored housing, pensions for the aged, social insurance, pure food and drug laws, limitation of hours of labor, especially for women and children, minimum wages, and laws condemning unsanitary and dangerous conditions in factories. At the same time he proposed government control of railroads, control of gas and electric power, coal and natural resources. Laissez faire capitalism, at its worst in the late nineteenth century, was designated "The Great Barbecue."

In advance of his times but reaffirming both Luther and Calvin was Rauschenbusch's emphasis on the Doctrine of Vocation. Its European counterpart included the many "Centers of New Life," such as Bad Boll in Germany, Sigtuna in Sweden, and Iona in Scotland. Rauschenbusch perceived that increasing emphasis on individualism supported a theology that de-emphasized human instrumentality. Far Eastern religions called the world evil and left it. A requirement for service of God is human accountability and responsibility. There is a strong element of contagion in such commitment. "When one person lights his torch at the altar of God, hundreds of persons will take their light from that person." Rauschenbusch's writings are filled with startling truths. "A selfish person becomes a stupid person if he lives long enough."

W. A. Visser 't Hooft in 1928 wrote his doctoral thesis on "The Background of the Social Gospel in America." Subsequently he became

General Secretary of the World Council of Churches. In 1957 on the 50th anniversary of the publication of Rauschenbusch's *Christianity and the Social Crisis* 't Hooft spoke at Colgate Rochester's Rauschenbusch Day. He spoke of the collision between the theologies of the Social Gospel and those which came from Germany in the post-war years. He said, "Now they have entered into a helpful and constructive discussion with each other and have both been transformed . . . The role of the structures of society is now recognized in the church . . . In the United States you are once again in a dangerous situation. The danger is that by the very size of the church . . . the church will fall into the great temptation of adjusting itself to its environment. In such a situation you will need to listen to prophetic voices, and to hear again the voice of Walter Rauschenbusch."[4]

To repeat again, the Social Gospel represents the first attempt on the part of religious leaders to correlate the rapidly emerging new insights in the physical and social sciences with higher criticism and the new biblical studies. The fact that so many clergymen of that period entered the newly emerging discipline of sociology is understandable. Sociology is the study of human relations, especially in group life manifestations. Significant figures turning from the ministry to sociology were William Graham Sumner, Albion W. Small, Charles A. Ellwood and others. Still other graduates of seminaries turned to psychology, though the seminal work of Freud had not yet given to psychology the same impetus which sociology provided. Later there were to emerge the names of Carl Rogers, Anton Boisen, Theodore M. Newcomb, et al.

The other major area previously mentioned which logically coincided with concerns of the Social Gospel was that of economics. Richard T. Ely (1854-1943) was to become in his time the University of Wisconsin's most widely known faculty member. He became the champion of the new historical school of economics, as well as protagonist of socialized Christianity. He gave scientific sanction to the criticism of classical economics. Ely went so far as to say that the Trades Union Movement was, next to the church, the strongest force in the world making for human brotherhood. He contended that half of the time of the theological student should be devoted to the social sciences and that theological seminaries should be the chief intellectual centers for sociology, which is concerned with the social consequences of sin.[5] Ely suggests that one of the indices of the thought of the church contributing to selfish individualistic piety is the kind of hymns sung in the church; "I and me are the recurring pronouns." In Ely's "Statement of Fundamental Beliefs in My Social Philosophy," he says candidly, "I am an aristocrat...not an aristocracy born for the enjoyment of special privilege, but an aristocracy which lives for the fulfillment of special service." This is especially significant coming from one of the giants of the Social Gospel Movement who influenced the economic thinking of so many clergymen.

Acceptance of the Social Gospel was the result of its breaking through the individualism and pietism which dominated so much of American church life. The doctrine of the Kingdom with its sense of social solidarity cracked the hypothesis of what many considered salvation. Interestingly, one of the books which appeared as the impact of the Social Gospel was diminishing was John Bennett's *Social Salvation* (1935). It appeared about the same time as Reinhold Niebuhr's *Moral Man and Immoral Society* (1934) which pointed to the emergence of other theological emphases.

INFLUENCE OF THE SOCIAL GOSPEL

In addition to emphasizing the Kingdom as a real possibility within history, the Social Gospel stressed also the immanence of God and the profound importance of man's worth. Robert Handy writes, "Though the church had long ago lost the true key to the Kingdom, now that key had been recovered. The spokesmen for the Social Gospel expected that through the efforts of men of good will the Kingdom of God would become a reality, bringing with it social harmony and the elimination of the worst social injustices. Thus the whole movement had something of a utopian cast." Corollary to the fundamental premise that the social principles of Jesus could serve as reliable guides for both individual and social life was the conviction that individuals could be educated to choose the good and develop their lives after the model of Jesus. If individuals would but will to do the good, they could bring it to pass. On this hypothesis much religious experimentation was undertaken and large scale organizational ventures were brought into being.

The early and widely disseminated Social Creed of the Churches (1908) owes its origin to the Social Gospel leadership in the Methodist Church. Around this Social Creed assembled leaders of other denominations, and it provided the core for the social thought of the newly forming Federal Council of Churches, also in 1908. Church leaders identified with the Social Creed entered into the 1919 steel strike in which the eight-hour day was one of the principal issues. Among other things the Creed called for was a "reasonable reduction of the hours of labor to the lowest practicable point." U.S. Steel bitterly resented church interference but the strike was won.

Most widely read but by no means the most profound piece of literature to come from the movement was Charles M. Sheldon's *In His Steps* (1896). The title carries the presuppositions of the movement. It is said to have had more copies printed than any other volume in the English language except the Bible. Each chapter constituted a sermon preached by Sheldon at his church in Topeka, Kansas, and describes the way individuals in various vocations followed in Jesus' footsteps. As a result thousands of individuals have sought to follow in their business or professional lives ways resembling those of Jesus. The idea had and still has a powerful hold on the will and imagination of many individuals.

Looking back on the period of the Social Gospel's greatest influence, two omissions stand out. They are war and race. The reasons for the omissions are apparent. The Civil War was a thing of the past. Brutal though it was, it had a "holy" purpose — to save the unity of the nation, and it freed slaves from bondage. It is significant that World War I coincided with the rapid decline of the Social Gospel. Though attempts were made to identify World War I as a holy crusade, and though the churches gave it substantial support, war came to be recognized by some of those who had been most active in the Social Gospel as basically wrong. After World War I Harry Emerson Fosdick, the best known liberal preacher of his day, announced, "I will never again bless another war." Following WWI a wave of pacifism emerged which was consistent with the underlying principles of the Social Gospel.

Why had not race been a more prominent issue? The Civil War had just been fought, and Negroes had been emancipated. Negro officials had been elected in Southern states and in the Congress. The harsh discrimination acts of the Southern states had not been enacted and the liberals of the North, with some exceptions such as Washington Gladden, felt that emancipation would assure justice for the black man. Not until the race riots in the North accompanying the large scale migrations to supply labor for World War I was the illusion concerning justice and opportunity for the black man exploded.

CONTEMPORARY MANIFESTATIONS

Rather than attempt to spell out implications of the Social Gospel for ministry in the contemporary world, I will instead cite briefly what some of our contemporaries are suggesting. Through them the reader may decide which emphases of the Social Gospel have been rejected, appropriated, modified, or transmogrified. I shall not place their judgments in exact juxtaposition to major emphases of the Social Gospel but rather permit the overtones of the contemporary emphases to speak to this similarity or dissimilarity.

A group calling themselves "The Younger Theologians" of a short generation ago, including Aubrey, Bennett, Cavert, Harkness, Horton, Pauck, Reinhold Niebuhr, Tillich, Van Dusen and others, shaped much of the thought of the Oxford and Amsterdam Conferences, according to Dean Thompson, writing recently in the *Christian Century*. "They discussed and wrote about problems confronting the Christian Church amid a setting of economic depression, crumbling international order and neo-orthodox revolt against the inadequacies of the Social Gospel liberalism."[6] The Oxford Conference adopted unofficially the slogan "Let the Church Be the Church," conveying the prophetic belief that the church occupies a unique relationship to the family, human work, the socio-economic order, the state and the international sphere. This group, augmented by others, fostered the development by the Federal Council of Churches of its Commission to Study the Bases of a Just and Durable Peace.

There is no single equivalent to that dubiously named group, "The Younger Theologians." Attempting something comparable for our own immediate period are two groups. One, composed of eighteen theologians, has issued "An Appeal for Theological Affirmation." This has become known as The Hartford Affirmation.[7] At the outset this Affirmation states, "Today an apparent loss of the sense of the transcendent is undermining the church's ability to address with clarity and courage the urgent tasks to which God calls it in the world." It rejects one of the cardinal issues in the Social Gospel, the acceptance of Jesus as a model, since this is likely to reflect cultural and countercultural notions of human excellence. It rejects the notion of human fulfillment as trivializing the promise. It rejects the idea of worship as promoting self-realization and human community. Worship is primarily a response to the reality of God. Much has been made in recent times of the need for the world to set the agenda for the church. The Affirmation contends that the church must help liberate the oppressed and heal misery, but the norms for the church's activity derive from its own perception of God's will for the world.

The other comtemporary statement, titled "The Boston Affirmations"[8] states in its Prologue, "We are concerned about what we discern to be present trends in our churches, in religious thought, and in society. We see struggles in every area of human life, but in too many parts of the church and theology we find retreat from these struggles." After a listing of doctrines and criteria which should inform our decisions and actions — such as Creation, Fall, New Covenant, Church Traditions — the Boston Affirmations raises the question under the caption, Present Witnesses, whether the heritage of the past can be sustained, preserved and extended into the future. These witnesses exemplify or discern the activity of God in such areas as struggles of the poor, the transforming drive for ethnic dignity, the efforts of many groups to develop a concern for the city, centers of civility, culture and human interdependence, and in the arts where beauty and meaning are explored. It closes with the comment, "On these grounds we cannot stand with those secular cynics and religious spiritualizers who see in such witness no theology, no eschatological urgency, and no godly promise or judgment."

Equally current with the two affirmations quoted above is another, but representing an even broader base of participants. It appears in "The Present State of the Discipline of Systematic Theology: A Preliminary

Report found in the Proceedings of the American Academy of Religion," 1975. The author, Thor Hall, received 580 responses from theologians who had been asked, among other questions, "What in your view is the main task facing the systematic theologian in the foreseeable future?" From the replies Hall discerns, "It is immediately apparent that theologians desire to speak to their own time, in a language, understandable in the present, and in ways that relate to the human situation and the contemporary world."[9] And he adds, that many of the theologians generalize on this point in terms of relating biblical faith and contemporary culture.

I wish I had the skill of a Burck, Bill Mauldin or a Herblock. I would portray Walter Rauschenbusch, Washington Gladden, Richard Ely, Graham Taylor and many others leaning over a cloud up yonder and watching what is happening currently down here. I think I can hear Saint Walter saying to his colleagues, "Gentlemen, this is where we came in."

NOTES

1. *An Interpretation of Christian Ethics* (N.Y. 1935), Preface.

2. For much of the information concerning Gladden the author is indebted to Robert Handy, *The Social Gospel in America* (N.Y.: Oxford University Press, 1966).

3. *A Theology for the Social Gospel*, 1918 passim, in *A Rauschenbusch Reader*, edited by Benson Y. Landis (N.Y.: Harper and Brothers, 1957).

4. Information Service, December 6, 1958.

5. See *Social Aspects of Christianity, and Other Essays*, c. 1889, quoted in Handy, *Social Gospel in America*.

6. *The Christian Century*, January 7, 1976.

7. "An Appeal for Theological Affirmation," *Worldview*, April 1975.

8. *The Boston Affirmations*, prepared by members of the Boston Industrial Mission Task Force and others, January 1976.

9. Reported in *The Christian Century*, March 17, 1976.

SUGGESTIONS FOR FURTHER READING

The Rise of the Social Gospel in American Protestantism by Charles Howard Hopkins (New Haven: Yale University Press, 1940). The most comprehensive documentation of the Social Gospel, its cultural and historical setting, leaders, fundamental ideas and accomplishments.

Protestant Churches and Industrial America by Henry F. May (N.Y.: Harper and Brothers, 1949), emphasizing the social and economic climate within which the Social Gospel emerged and had its influence.

The Social Gospel in America by Robert T. Handy (N.Y.: Oxford University Press, 1966). Excellent summaries and analyses of the three Social Gospel pioneers, Gladden, Ely, Rauschenbusch.

A Rauschenbusch Reader compiled by Benson Y. Landis (N.Y.: Harper and Brothers, 1957) with an interpretation of the life of Walter Rauschenbusch by Harry Emerson Fosdick.

A lifelong student of Walter Rauschenbusch selects the heart of his message from his greatest works.

Graham Taylor, Pioneer for Social Justice by Louise C. Wade (Chicago: University of Chicago Press, 1964). The life of one who expressed in many creative forms the rationale and motivation of the Social Gospel. Of special interest to those who know CTS and Chicago.

The Social Gospel Re-Examined by Ernest F. Johnson (N.Y.: Harper and Brothers, 1940). The Rauschenbusch Lectures at Colgate-Rochester Seminary. An evaluation of social and theological thought following the Social Gospel period and emerging from it.

In His Steps by Charles M. Sheldon, no copyright, many publishers. Of interest as a phenomenon of its period for its influence on religious thought and action of countless thousands.

LIBERATION 200 YEARS ON

By J. ROBERT MEYNERS

Among the several skeletons in the closet of the American Church is a certain eighteenth century revolution. It is impossible to join in this year of national celebration without remembering our origins in a war of revolt against constituted political authority. This can be rather embarrassing. We ourselves are now the rich and powerful, the objects of other people's revolutionary scorn. We are surrounded by movements of liberation which threaten to embroil us in uncomfortable controversies both political and theological

One way to deal with this embarrassment is to romanticize the revolution, remembering Paul Revere riding in the night and Betsy Ross sewing on brightly colored bunting. But the decision to defect from British suzerainty was fraught with tragic controversy. Florida and the Canadian provinces refused to fight the British. Congregationalists in Massachusetts were deeply divided on the war. With few exceptions the Church of England and its clergy remained loyalists. John Wesley wrote no less than thirteen tracts against the rebel cause, precipitating a rift with his American followers. All revolutions, including our own, are complicated, confusing and full of social, political and moral ambiguity.

However, if by some deft achievement of historical fantasy we were to remember the revolution as a moral consensus, we would have two hundred more years to reinterpret. We would have to suppress the suspicion that the revolutionary spirit was not only an originating event, but also a continuing part of our national character. We would have to forget that this spirit continued to emerge in the struggles over slavery, for the right of women to vote, in the rise of the labor movement, and in a never ending series of controversial Constitutional amendments.

The church has often sought to transcend political controversies but it has seldom managed to remain completely aloof. We cannot live **down** our revolutionary heritage. Neither can we **live off** our past. Apparently Jefferson was right in claiming that every generation must agonize through its own revolution.

The revolutionary spirit is abroad in the world today in movements and idealogies of **liberation.** Blacks, women, and dispossessed people of the earth are increasingly engaged in this struggle. These pages are written in the belief that we can fail to take these movements seriously only by performing a self-inflicted lobotomy in which we cut out the memory of our national origins and subsequent history.

What is liberation? What is oppression? These are questions which history now presses upon every conscientious Christian, calling into question our achievements, our lifestyle, our values, our future. We cannot expect to agree upon our responses, but the demand for response is relentless. The geographical areas now emerging into a self-conscious struggle for freedom from misery hold the majority of the earth's people. The entire world could become one vast "Rhodesia" with an embattled minority living in a fool's paradise, pretending the day of redress is not at hand.

It has become increasingly obvious that theologians and religious leaders cannot tell the rest of us what opinions we should hold. Advice even on questions of private morality is less than fully welcome. This should not come as any modern surprise. Important as the great fathers of the church were to the development of a Christian ethos, it was the churches and the people who made up the churches who first heard the gospel, sifted through its conflicting messages and responded finally with the firmness of faith.

While the church is inevitably divided within itself regarding current liberation movements and theologies, religious leaders can find ways of facilitating the Christian community's search for the relation of their faith to the enterprise of human liberation. In these pages I want to call attention to some important facets of liberation theology, point to some principles by which persons and congregations can clarify their faith in relation to these issues, and then provide a typical example of the use of this methodology.

SOME KEY ISSUES IN LIBERATION THEOLOGIES

Our purpose here is to illustrate a method of dealing with issues, and not to give an intellectual exercise on the nature of liberation theology. Thus the following paragraphs are simply statements of three of the critical issues raised for the entire church by liberation perspectives.

1. *The Gospel is a gospel of liberation from oppression.* The Bible is the story of liberation, starting with the Hebrew people's constant struggle to be free from external domination and the internal oppression of sin and faithlessness. The Bible has a virtual prejudice on the side of the poor, the weak, the slave, the widow, the fatherless, the stranger at the gate. When Jesus began his ministry he read in the synagogue from Isaiah:

> The spirit of the Lord is upon me, because he has annointed me to preach good news to the poor. He has sent me to proclaim release to the captives and the recovering of sight to the blind, to set at liberty those who are oppressed, to proclaim the acceptable year of the Lord (Luke 4: 18-19).

And Paul preached the freedom of those who are saved in Christ from the "law of sin and death".

The task of liberation theology is to illuminate the nature of oppression and to discover anew the nature of the liberating promise. Liberation theologies include such diversity as Gutierrez's class analysis and Mary Daly's caste system (as well as) Charles Long's black folk religion and James Cone's black power. For all of them, oppression comes from the outside in social and political structures and from the inside in personal and religious attitudes. The poor and the powerless cooperate in their own oppression, feeling themselves worthless and guilty and deserving of their suffering. Similarly the powerful internalize the oppressed, seeing themselves as powerless to change the system and excusing themselves as virtual victims of a structure they did not create.

2. *The Gospel is a gospel of particularity.* Liberation theologians speak fully and finally out of their own particular experience as oppressed. Instead of doing "theology", they are doing black theology or Latin theology or they are doing Christian theology "from a feminine perspective." They are not concerned with theology in general. This is the radical affirmation that the experience of oppression is a unique source of revelatory reflection. It is the claim that something is learned from oppression that has not been and cannot be learned in any other way. Some will put this so radically as to claim that only the oppressed can develop Christian theology.

This has appeared as a scandal to those of us who want Christianity to have a universal message for all people. We have of course recognized that our religious attitudes are culturally conditioned and that we must remember the partial character of all our perceptions of truth. However, we have usually regarded that as a problem to be overcome. We must strive to know universal truth. It is therefore shocking to have theologians ignoring or frankly disparaging this universalism and affirming that the only Christian truth available to us is that which emerges when the word of God comes to us in our particular situation of suffering and shame.

Thus many black theologians are writing first of all for black people and only secondarily for others who may wish to listen in. This raises critical questions for white middle-class Christians: Is there a gospel of liberation for us? Are we oppressed? If so, what is the nature of our oppression? Or are we only oppressors? Is there a liberating word for those of us whose oppression is largely a matter of cooperating in other people's oppression?

119

3. *The Gospel is a gospel of ecclesial action.* Liberation theology is addressed to the communal and personal responsibility of Christians. The people of God are understood as those who struggle against oppression, in themselves, in others and in social structures. Brothers and sisters in Christ are not identified by church membership but by participation in the struggle. Gutierrez defines theology as "critical reflection on ecclesial praxis".

There is a subtle but profound difference between this view and a liberal gospel of social action. In the latter the church is understood as making judgments about social existence based on its faith and accordingly entering into the political process to influence it. Liberation theology by contrast sees the church as a social institution which by its very presence participates in the structures which oppress. The model of intervention ordinarily used commits us to one or another secular model of social change. The alternative is that the people themselves engage in the process which Freire has dubbed "conscienticization". This is a massive exercise in personal and social awareness by which people reflect on their own experience, begin to trust their own perceptions, reject the notion that suffering is deserved and begin to project participation in the structures of power.

Liberation theology may therefore not concern itself first with questions about epistemology or ontology. The first question is what are the people of God about? How are they involved in oppression, their own and that of other people? How are they embodying the liberating word in the world? Then the nature of God's being, the person and the world are meaningfully addressed, not as intellectual questions, but as questions of passionate concern on which liberation as salvation depends.

TOWARD A METHODOLOGY OF CLARIFICATION

How can we deal with the issues raised by liberation theology without assuming prophetic or ecclesiastical authority? How can we facilitate the process by which people in our churches deal creatively with controversial issues? A theory for doing this is given in *Values and Teaching* by Louis Raths, Merrill Harmin and Sidney Simon (Columbus, O.: Charles E. Merrill, 1966). Here are some operational principles drawn from the theory of values clarification and addressed to questions of faith and action. Hortatory in form, they will be most useful if religious leaders revise and complete them for themselves, providing more specific content in the light of their own particular situations.

1. *Emphasize the valuing process.* Let the emphasis be not on judging the conclusions to which other people come, but on the process by which persons and groups within the church struggle with their own consciences in the community of faith.

120

2. *Begin with the faith and values people do in fact already have.* Persons are not blank tablets on which a faith can be inscribed. It is important to help people to get in touch with the faith they already hold (Christian, civic, cultural, private). To ignore these values is to court disruptive conflict.

3. *Facilitate consideration of alternatives to values already held.* A value is not a value until it is considered and chosen freely from among alternatives which might have been selected. The church can be a place and an atmosphere in which people may struggle with agonizing controversial issues without fear of being disrespected.

4. *Encourage both the affective and cognitive elements to enter the valuing process.* Both thought and feeling are important dimensions of the decisions of faith. We can find ways of respecting both elements while alternatives are freely considered.

5. *Design methods of interaction that bring out personal and sub-group responses.* Even discussion methods are often over-powering to people with low self-confidence or weak communication skills. Privacy of belief may be important at some stages of decision.

6. *Provide opportunities for people to proclaim their values.* A value is not a value unless we are willing under some appropriate circumstances to publicly affirm what we believe. The early church recognized the importance of witness and testimony. A witness is not something which others are invited to argue with. An appropriate response by the hearers is "Amen", not necessarily in agreement, but by way of saying "I hear you."

7. *Encourage action congruent with the faith and values affirmed.* A value is not really a value unless it is acted upon, and, indeed it is not a value when it is acted upon only once or twice. A position becomes a deeply cherished conviction at the point where it is acted upon with relative consistency over time.

8. *Claim the right to your own convictions.* The process here suggested does not ask leaders to abdicate their own conviction or passion. In fact it requires that leaders reveal themselves, if only for the sake of objectivity, since the way leaders develop the process will be influenced by their biases.

9. *Expect the graceful event of Christian community.* Christian faith is fulfilled in a life together where in the struggle with one another and with the world, we become a community of faith and action. In active expectancy we can wait upon this graceful event, persistent in our efforts to remove the blocks, patient in the hope that it may occur among us, confident in our faith that the promise will be fulfilled.

Now let us assume the burdens of local religious leadership in relation to liberation theology. The earlier paragraphs on liberation theology are drastic over-simplifications of a vast literature. They are still unsuited for direct use in the pulpit or an adult education class. Of course these ideas could be simplified even further: translate the translation into language and images which will connect with the experience of people in the church. Apart from the genius of a pastor or leader this will be hopelessly inadequate. First it will be inadequate because it is doing the theological task for the people, rather than engaging them in the process itself. Second, it will be inadequate because of the inadequacy of the translation. The experience of oppression out of which liberation theologians have written cannot be embodied in the words of a white-anglo-saxon-male-who-is-not-poor. So let us see what would happen if we try to design some experiential strategies which employ some of these principles and seek to connect with these issues.

Let us assume an opening session in an adult education class, in which there will be from time to time some content in-put by the leader as a part of the on-going process over several weeks, and that strategies like we have mentioned will be developed around that content and related to the particular faith issues that emerge in the group.

Strategy I — Purpose: To help people get in touch with the feeling of oppression and the hope of liberation in their own lives and to give some content to these words.

Use the following or similar words: "Let's see what may happen if we 'free associate' around the words 'oppression' and 'liberation'. I am going to move around the room and say Oppression is. . .' and I will point to someone. If I point to you, say the first word that comes into your mind. Don't try to be profound. Just say whatever comes into your mind." Now the leader moves around the room pointing to one person after the other, moving quickly. If someone cannot or does not say anything, have a variety of responses ready, like "Oppression is me asking you to say what oppression is." After a few minutes switch back to the word "oppression" but this time, after you have gotten a response, say to the next person, "If oppression is (what the last person had said) then liberation is. . .". Thus if one person were to respond "Oppression is hating my job," the leader would say, "If oppression is hating my job, then liberation is. . ." and point to another person for a completion response.

This strategy works well in a group where people are already fairly comfortable with one another. It can also be enjoyable and help people to open up to one another. Spend a few minutes talking about what happened. Be sensitive to the possibility that people may have felt a little manipulated and bring this out in the open. The feeling of being gently oppressed here and now can be a useful connector to other experiences of more serious oppression.

Alternatives to this strategy can be devised if the group is tense or uncomfortable with one another. The leader can prepare a written set of alternative completions that follow the same pattern, permitting people to explore their thought and feelings in privacy. Another alternative is to have people make drawings or other non-verbal representations of oppression and liberation and then discuss these in small groups.

Strategy II — Purpose: To allow participants to be more emotionally in touch with the suffering of people for whom oppression is a present and horrible reality. (This will work best if the leader writes an original fantasy).

Instructions: "I am going to ask you to follow my words into a fantasy. Let your imagination fill-in the picture as I describe it to you. Close your eyes if you wish. Let your mind enter into the scene." (Speak slowly, pausing between sentences).

Fantasy: "Imagine yourself to be among the wretched of the earth. You are in a damp abandoned basement room with several others, an old man, a gaunt mother, two small children. It is bitterly cold. There have been only a few scraps of food for days. You huddle together, strangers under some filthy, shredding blankets. Presently you get up and go out to the cellar-way because there is no water and no toilet. You come back in and scramble under the blankets to find that the two-year old has been sick where you lay before. You nurse the pain of nausea and hunger in your belly.

"Suddenly the door bursts open and a drunken man lunges at the mother, beating and choking her. The children scream, you are petrified. You grab a stick and beat the man off. Blood is over his face as he staggers out the door, muttering his hatred for the woman and you. You go back to your place under the blanket. In your misery you turn toward the wall. Through tears of pain and anger you see some words scratched dimly on the wall: JESUS SAVES."

Allow a few minutes of silence, and perhaps a prayer. "For the obscenity of looking at other's suffering, Forgive us. For the futility of looking away from other's suffering, Forgive us. From the arrogance of excusing ourselves, deliver us. From the sentimentality of excusing others, deliver us. Call us to share the burden of suffering, not only in imagination but in fact." Allow some time for the sharing of responses to the experience, being sensitive to any discomfort or even anger which may be present. Emphasize the inadequacy of the fantasy in identifying with other's suffering, which defies the power of our imagination.

123

With these two exercises in the background, the leader may wish to outline one or two ideas that have emerged out of liberation theology, for example, the notion of the internalized oppressor. Or if the participants have read some material on liberation theology, this would be a time to discuss this.

Strategy III— Purpose: To look at some alternative styles of liberation often urged on oppressed persons.

Instructions: Place the following or similar words on four large pieces of newsprint and fasten them around the walls.

Bootstrap Model: Everyone is responsible for him/herself. There are resources available, opportunities for advancement. No one needs to be poor or oppressed. Hard work and initiative pay off.

Lifehook Model: The poor and oppressed cannot help themselves because they do not have the means. Only the rich and powerful by sharing their resources can alleviate the misery of weak and hopeless people.

Quilting Bee Model: Cooperation between the powerful and the oppressed is the way progress takes place. Everyone will recognize that their own self-interest lies in the direction of equal justice for all. This can best be achieved by working together.

Street Gang Model: There will be no change unless oppressed people organize and enforce their rights. No one gives up power and privilege voluntarily.

Use the following or similar words: "This is basically a game and we will no doubt enjoy fooling around with some ideas behind which there is a quite serious problem. We have purposely used overly simplified statements, and we will ask you to make each of these strategies sound as plausible as possible." (Divide the participants arbitrarily into four groups and assign each group to one of the four points of view.) "You will be given fifteen minutes to caucus, to choose a spokesperson, and to instruct that person on the arguments the group wants to use. Use as many religious arguments as possible. When the fifteen minutes is up, each spokesperson will have five minutes to argue that perspective."

Strategy IV — Purpose: To give people something to take home with them and continue to reflect at leisure and in privacy. The issues raised in this way can be drawn from the content issues already introduced in the leader's presentation, or used to raise new issues which may be dealt with in an ensuing session. As the participants leave, give each person the following written exercise:

> Consider each of the following five statements and think about your agreement or disagreement. Then rank the statements from the one you agree with most to the one you agree with least.

1. Christian religious ideas are, or should be, universal truths and do not represent the biases of any class or group.

2. Christian religious ideas today represent largely middle-class values that are not useful to the poor and oppressed.

3. Christian ideas have been partly perverted to the selfish interests of wealth and power and therefore for the good of all, we need to reinterpret ideas in ways that enhance the struggle of those who are oppressed.

4. Christian ideas are deeply influenced by the social and economic condition of those who hold them, but there are elements in the gospel which transcend selfish interests.

5. The poor and oppressed need to develop a Christian theology of their own, independent of the traditional ideas that are especially the possession of those who are not poor.

When you have finished, ponder your reasons. Reflect on the consequences of your opinion. What biases, if any, do you find in yourself? Would you expect poor people to believe as you do? If not, why? Do your emotions and your ideas go in different directions?

All four of these strategies are offered as examples of methods which can be used to raise controversial issues in the church and in a way that can introduce creative disagreement. The range of possible strategies is as broad as the imagination of the leader. The examples given here will have served a useful purpose only if readers are encouraged to develop strategies reflective of their own creativity and the uniqueness of the situations in which they exercise leadership.

BIBLIOGRAPHY

Cecil Wayne Cone, *The Identity Crisis in Black Theology* (Nashville: MEC Press, 1975).

Paulo Freire, *Pedagogy of the Oppressed* (New York: Seabury, 1970).

Gustavo Gutierrez, *A Theology of Liberation* (Maryknoll, N.Y.: Orbis Books, 1971).

Frederick Herzog, *Liberation Theology* (New York: Seabury Press, 1972).

Letty M. Russell, *Human Liberation in a Feminist Perspective* (Philadelphia: Westminister, 1974).

Sidney B. Simon, Leland W. Howe, and Howard Kirschenbaum. *Values Clarification: A Handbook of Practical Strategies for Teachers and Students* (New York: Hart, 1972).

CHURCH ADMINISTRATION AND THE HUMAN POTENTIAL MOVEMENT

By PHILIP A. ANDERSON

Church administration is caring for the whole congregation in such a way as to enable the increase of the love of God, the love of neighbor and the love of self. Often ministers have thought that the word administration referred to a special form of work which stood alongside other kinds of work, e. g., preaching, counseling, and teaching. This distinction may be useful for distinguishing certain aspects of the life of the congregation, but it is too limiting. D. V. Donnison in the book *Social Policy and Administration* says that for the serious student of the subject, "Administration should include **all** the activities and influences that determine the character and outcome of the tasks he [the serious student] is studying. He is interested in **all** [emphasis mine] who participate in these processes and contribute to their outcome — whether or not they happen to be called 'administrators' and whether or not they are employed by the agency whose work is being studied" (40-41).

By church administration then, I mean the totality of the tasks, the processes, the influences, and the persons which make up the life of a congregation.

The human potential movement has grown out of and draws upon many of the theories and the practices of various fields of thought in humanistic psychology — psychosynthesis, bioenergetics, gestalt therapy, transactional analysis, structural integration. Its goal is the self actualization of persons.

Humanistic psychology takes an optimistic view of human nature. The human being is essentially good; societal pressures and stresses coupled with his perception of them have distorted or deformed his nature. In theological terms, the person is made in the image of God and called to be whole even as the father in heaven is **whole** (a more accurate translation of **perfect**).

What does the human potential movement have to say to church administration? The theory and methods of gestalt therapy, one of the fields of the human potential movement, suggest proposals for a style of church administration that will make real the love which the church proclaims. Let us look at some of the basic understandings and practices of gestalt therapy.

A gestalt is a pattern, a configuration, the particular organization of the individual parts. The basic premise of gestalt psychology is that human nature is organized into patterns or wholes, that the world is experienced by the individual in these terms, and that life can only be understood as a function of the patterns or wholes of which it is made.

Persons perceive themselves and their environment as a gestalt at any given moment. Each person organizes his or her world into a gestalt and lives as a whole person, not as a collection of fragmented parts, such as mind and body and legs and experiences. Persons maintain their equilibrium through a process called homeostasis. When new experiences emerge in the environment or when the person becomes aware of hidden aspects in themselves, then the person feels upset or incomplete and seeks a new gestalt which will organize their world again. All life is characterized by this continuing play of balance and imbalance, completeness and incompleteness, equilibrium and disequilibrium, need and fulfillment of need. The person's gestalt is upset by some new need within the self or the environment. A struggle goes on to find a new gestalt.

A person becomes aware of hunger pains while writing at a desk. His gestalt has been centered around the writing of a paper. Now the center shifts to the hunger pains which have upset the writing gestalt. The person moves to the refrigerator and equilibrium is reestablished by eating. Persons are in a never-ending struggle for the strongest gestalt which will organize the world of the self and its environment into a meaningful whole. If the person blocked out or ignored or did not let himself become aware of the hunger pains for a long enough period, he would die.

But there is great common sense in us. We become aware of fundamental needs and reorganize our current gestalt to find a new equilibrium. We change in small ways and sometimes in large ways when we let ourselves be aware of some new or hidden part within us or in our world, and reorganize our gestalt to take account of that part. The gestalt process of change happens when we see some new part of our psychophysical world as the figure or center and allow the rest of our inner and outer world to become background. In the above example, the center shifted from a paper in a typewriter to the hunger pain. The person then acted on the basis of this new gestalt and went to the refrigerator.

Right now as you are reading this each one of you is organizing and reorganizing your gestalt depending upon what is central for you. My words or a word may be the centering focus for you. My voice or my appearance may be the center. Or you may be organizing your gestalt around some center from your home church. You face some administrative problem at home, say a very angry member of your board of trustees, and he is the organizing center of your gestalt as you read this. Everything I say is being fitted into your gestalt in relation to that angry man or woman center. Meanwhile that angry man's gestalt centers around the declining income of the church and the unrealistic budget. He is organizing his gestalt around that center.

A person's gestalt is constantly changing as he or she becomes aware of other parts of the world. What is this process of change? How does it happen? As church persons we are interested in change.

Change occurs when persons let go and allow themselves to become **aware** of what is happening in the here and now of their world by utilizing all of their senses. This paying attention, awareness, allows a new center to emerge and thus change the person's gestalt. You might become aware of the angry person's overriding concern for the church, his passion, which is larger than his immediate anger about the budget. And as you centered on his passion you would see him in a new light, allowing you to make **contact** with him in a fresh way. You would have changed some of your assumptions about him. And any change in your center, or assumptions, changes the gestalt, sometimes in tiny ways, but the new gestalt is different.

Awareness is the beginning point. Right now you can experiment with this awareness power for yourself. Stop reading and centering on this paper. Pay attention to the here and now where you are by saying "Here and now I see the window, here and now I see _____." Do this for two minutes. Now shift your attention and say "Here and now I touch _____ and it feels _____." Do this for two minutes. Now shift your attention and say, "Here and now I hear _____." Do this for two minutes. What happened as you paid attention to the here and now of your world? Did your center change as you became more aware of your world through your senses?

Most of the research on the power of awareness has come from work with individuals in gestalt therapy. The following case illustrates the power of the process. We will then consider its potential for the church system.

I offered the "here and now" experiment to a man who came to see me recently. His stomach was heaving and knotted. He was angry at the authorities controlling his life including his parents whose controls he still felt though they had been dead for some years. They were to blame for urging him into the profession he now found intolerable. He told his story with a tight, pained face, through gritted teeth. After his initial explosion, I asked him to do this here and now exercise, to become aware of what and how he was touching, feeling, seeing now. After three or four minutes his face relaxed. He became intrigued with seeing and touching some of the common objects in my office. I asked him, then, "How is your stomach now?"

To his great surprise he said, "Quiet and easy." And I was reminded of Jesus' words: "Behold, now is the acceptable time; behold, now is the day of salvation." The past is our heritage. The future needs planning. But to live in the past, or out of the past and to live in the future of not yets, is to miss the only possible time, namely **now** in which we can take responsibility to act or touch or see or smell or hear or taste or think.

We know how to enable a person to find a new equilibrium in his gestalt. The gestalt process has much to say to us about the church also. The church is a gestalt infinitely more complex than a single person's gestalt, having many more parts — members, building, location, denomination. Churches maintain their equilibrium through the same homeostatic process as persons do. Administration is the facilitating of that process. When new experiences or parts emerge in the church, there is upset, disequilibrium and struggle until some new centering emerges and a new gestalt is created, a new equilibrium established. The process is never-ending.

The gestalt process suggests the necessity of becoming aware of the parts in the life of a person or in the life of a congregation and binding them back together again, performing the ministry of reconciliation. To enable such a process is to enable the fundamental experience of religion. The word "religion" (**religare**) means "to bind," "to bind back," "to bind together," "to be concerned."

The increase of awareness in ourselves and in others is a valuable skill in church administration. Let us explore this further.

One way to develop awareness, a way I have already described, is to focus on the present moment, to value it, act in it, enjoy it. Emerson observed that nature always lives in the present, not subject to either the disappointments of the past or the anxieties of the future.

> These roses under my window make no reference to former roses or to better ones; they are for what they are; they exist with God today. There is not time to them. There is simply the rose; it is perfect in every moment of its existence...but man [and woman] postpones and remembers. He cannot be happy and strong until he, too, lives with nature in the present, above time.

Consider now how much of our time spent in church administration is concerned with the past. We work over the biblical story of the paralytic without letting ourselves be aware of how **we are paralyzed** ourselves right now. We rehearse our heritage of bondage being overcome in Egypt, in the Pauline churches, in the South of slavery days, in the resistance movement of the war, in the stories of men and women of all ages, but we do now allow ourselves to become aware of the bondage we sense in ourselves and in the church right now. We preach the good news of resurrection overcoming crucifixion and death, but we block sharing awareness of how dead or alive we feel right now. We rehearse past budgets, programs, buildings, and the attendant successes and failures, but we do not share what we are aware of now — excitement, anxiety, fear, pain, joy, our behavior now.

Likewise, much of our administration of the congregation is future oriented. We plan programs. We anticipate events. We raise budgets. We act as though we believe that bigger is better, and since we are in the business of becoming better, we spend much of our time and energy in a search to become bigger, reach more people, take in new members, rejuvenate the church school.

Some future planning is necessary of course; an alive church cannot do without it. So is some awareness of the past necessary; a strong church is strengthened by being able to look at its roots. But, when concern for the past (tradition) and anxiety about the future affect the church's response to the present, when the angry man remains angry, the dreamer continues to dream, the hurt ones and the joyous ones share neither their hurt or their joy — in short, when the church is stuck in the same old past-or-future patterns, a conscious valuing of the present moment is called for.

One of the simplest ways to pay attention to the present moment is to ask the members of a study group or a board, or a committee to go around, and report, "Right now I am aware _____." When I do this with any kind of group I am working with, the gestalt invariably changes — sometimes dramatically, sometimes slightly — but the gestalt is new. Disequilibrium occurs. A different center emerges. The group finds a new gestalt encompassing factors which were previously hidden. If, on the other hand, I let the group go on in its own way, each person speaking out of their past or their future, the gestalt tends to remain the same.

Recently I was working with the board of directors of a church-related agency which found itself in difficulty. For the first hour we heard nothing but stories about our glorious past, interspersed with questions from several members who knew the right radical change we needed for survival. Everybody was speaking from their own gestalt which they had brought to the all-day session.

I asked them to stop and go around the group telling us what they were aware of right now. The gestalt began to change when the third person said, "Right now I'm aware of my fear that I might fail our agency." The next person said, "Right now I'm aware of my frustration. I'm aware of how helpless I feel." So it went. Awareness of sadness, fear, helplessness. I began to feel all of this myself. How and what could I do about all of this negativity? Maybe I should not have started this process. And then my faith in awareness was restored when one of the members said, "Somehow I feel better knowing how all of you really feel right now even though the feelings are heavy. I thought I was the only one. I'm not alone anymore and knowing that makes me believe we can change it." The board members all laughed with a rush of agreement. They had reported just how it was now, the center changed and the gestalt changed. Each member had taken responsibility for where he or she was right now.

Reality is different from the assumptions we make. There was real grimness in the reality facing this board. But they could act now knowing how they really were, not assuming that the others had it together or that the truth was too difficult. The awareness exercise of going around enabled them to know more of the reality of their sadness, fear and helplessness. They could care for themselves and for the organization on a more realistic basis. One could sense the improved morale in the new gestalt.

As administrator you are part of the gestalt which is the church. If you choose to enable awareness in the church system you should be warned that you cannot manipulate the outcome. Letting persons own and take responsibility for what they are aware of right now cannot be controlled. But becoming aware lets new gestalts emerge. Letting myself become aware of parts of my world which I have not focused on before is to work out my salvation with fear and trembling, and discover my excitement and energy for action.

How can a pastor heighten the awareness of the persons in the congregation on a Sunday morning? There are many ways. You will discover that you are very inventive once you've accepted awareness as one of your goals. Let me tell you of one method I have used.

Recently I was invited to spend a weekend with a large congregation, to meet with several small groups and boards on Saturday and to preach at two services to some 500 persons on Sunday. Concerned about awareness, I enabled an increase of awareness with the small groups on Saturday. On Sunday, I preached from the text reporting Jesus' visit to his home town and the subsequent resentment of his wisdom. Jesus left without performing miracles. The text makes clear that the people knew about Jesus' healing power. I suggested to the congregation that it might have been different if the home folks had let themselves be aware and reported to Jesus not only their resentment but also their appreciation.

Then I offered the members of the congregation the opportunity to go on a personal, guided fantasy trip. They could close their eyes or day dream if they wished, but I wanted them to have the chance to become aware of their resentments and appreciations. I guided them in their imagination to the people they live with — parents, children, spouses — and suggested they go in their imagination to one of them and tell him what they appreciated about the person and to listen for any response. I was silent for 30 seconds. Subsequently I took them to a person in the church, a person where they work, a person from their past, a person in the world beyond their acquaintanceships, and then to the road outside of Nazareth where they would meet Jesus coming out of the town. "Tell Jesus what you appreciate about him and wait for any response." Each time there was 30 seconds of silence. Finally, I suggested that they tell themselves what they appreciated about themselves. And that was the end of the sermon.

I was unprepared for the response. People were thoughtful, some of them were crying, others were quite astonished by what they had discovered about the appreciation stored in them and unexpressed. The minister told me later that immediately after the service he observed people making their way to other persons in the church and telling them about how they appreciated them. Awareness transformed some of the relationships. The gestalt of that church changed a little.

The gestalt process of church administration goes like this: first, The church is a **gestalt**; second, **awareness** upsets the equilibrium of that gestalt; third, through increased awareness, dialogue, contact, movement, taking responsibility, a **new center** emerges; fourth, a new gestalt is formed.

Another powerful and simple way to enable the church to become increasingly aware is to encourage the members to pay attention to their language. Suggest to a meeting of the church council, for example, that the members pay attention to what they say and how they say it. Notice, particularly, where the responsibility lies. First, ask them to **personalize their pronouns,** by changing "it" to "I," "you" to "I," and "we" to "I." I remember council members saying, "We are not taking in enough new members. We are not greeting people warmly and recognizing new faces." When changed to "I am not greeting people warmly and I am not recognizing new faces," there was a new awareness for that person of the extent to which he or she was willing to take responsibility for what was going on in the church system. The language of the church council frequently abounds with assumptions about "you," "it" and "we."

Second, encourage the council members to become aware of how they use verbs. "We can't change the worship service" is literally not true. We can. The sentence properly translates into, "I won't let the worship be changed." Taking responsibility for what I will do and what I won't do makes for honesty and directness of communication. **Can't** frequently means **won't.**

"We **have to** run an every member canvas this year" has a heavy, "ought" sound to it. Encourage the council to own their choice, "We **choose to** run an every member canvas" or "We choose not to run an every member canvas" is to realize that we do have choice at most every moment.

Become aware of the many assumptions the council members make about the other members around the table and in the church. "I know that everybody was unhappy with the conduct of the Maundy Thursday communion service this year." Such a statement makes the minister, the deacons and everybody else run for cover. Check the language. How does the person know that? Perhaps the statement is impossible. The pastor-administrator can ask the person to try the sentence, "I was unhappy with the communion service" and then to **check out** his experience with others around the council table. Many people jump to conclusions, assuming they know what the others think and feel, when they can only imagine.

A third language shift has to do with **"ands"** and **"buts."** A council member says, "I want the minister to have a sabbatical, but we cannot afford it." The "but" takes away the affirmation of the first clause. The "after-the-but-statement" is remembered and often carries the argument. Ask the speaker to change the "but" to "and." What happens? "I want the minister to have a sabbatical and I am not sure we can afford it." Now the affirmation remains and the financial issue can be seen in its proper perspective.

Another sentence change which enhances awareness is to ask the council members to change their **questions** to **statements.** What is the statement behind your question? "What do you think about sabbaticals for pastors?" leaves the members of a pastoral relations committee wondering and anxious. "I want the minister to have a sabbatical" lets them respond to a position. Questions keep putting the responsibility on the other person instead of taking responsibility for yourself and owning where you stand.

A fourth language shift, suggests that we ask **"how"** and **"what"** instead of **"why."** Why seeks for causes, and tracing causality can be an endless and often inconclusive search. "Why didn't you like the communion service?" can be translated into "What was going on? How was the service being conducted? What did you experience?" The answers will be far more specific.

A final administering of language awareness has to do with increasing personal awareness of the **use of qualifiers** such as "may," "possibly," "might," "if only," "try." All of these qualifiers allow us to hedge our bets.

They are not in line with the biblical call to let our "yes" be "yes" and our "no," "no." "I'll try to call on the new member," often hides the real feeling: "I won't but I also won't tell you that now." And the new member does not receive a call.

In all of these language shifts we can as administrators enable increased awareness and responsibility in the church system. A new style for enabling the purpose of the church can emerge in our congregations. The gestalt process gives administrators new tools for empowering the church, not for controlling the church. When awareness is enabled and new gestalts appear, excitement, surprise, and energy emerge. When and where you least expect it, grace may appear.

A MODEL OF LEADERSHIP IN A CONGREGATION

By ROSS SNYDER

We are forever in need of persons capable of leading on the religious enterprise of our civilization.

There is widespread feeling in our country that we have never before had such **technically** able persons in the various professions. But we have few who can speak the words and enact the acts which the members of that profession (and the rest of us) would follow into new humanness and moral aboundingness. As citizens we do not see that any of the great professions will provide enough **morale** leadership to their own group, let alone to the ways a society can take on the humankind-building that profession is supposed to lead.

As citizens we see those who aspire to political leadership of our country as makers of clever words and projectors of "image of the week." And manipulators of the rest of us for the self-interest groups who contribute the campaign funds and deliverable voters.

And as for ourselves personally, we are each too exclusively attending to individualistic profit-taking, comforting ourselves with pleasures, "realizing" our potential, our consumer desires, **our** encaved values. We mean to maintain dominion . . . and on our own present terms. Our homes give our children all kinds of gifts except that of the experience of being a family. And so do our marriages.

And yet people in the new field of psychohistory are discovering that all over the world, some persons live as human dignity and love in the very midst of disastrous social conditions. And further, in their living, they are working out the problems their society must transcend. Out of what resources do they live?

Looking at the churches, we would report that there is no theologian or religious leader of the established churches whose interpretative skill is widely respected. Positively we are wondering if the local congregation isn't a much more important possibility for life than the brain-washing which pop culture and "prophetic" church leadership has put us through for about twenty years. Maybe the **congregation is an essential** of democratic culture. And of personal existence through the years of our life.

Maybe we have been too unable in bringing off **spirited congregation**. And have not even been focused in doing so.

Increasing numbers of people are becoming determined that there should be an end to this wide-ranging void of quality and power to lead on the American enterprise of humankind. But today the custom is to rush to day-and-a-half training sessions and short-term counselling to improve technical skills and the size of vocabulary with which one can defend the **being** which he already unfortunately is. All we need are a few more insertions into the instrumental regions of our leadership of humanity's journey through wilderness.

But leadership is a so much larger matter.

This paper comes with a long-term fascination for the leadership team of four men who were central in the Pilgrim venture at Plymouth . . . William Bradford, John Robinson, William Brewster, Henry Ainsworth. Incurably, common Americans have believed that there is something in the Pilgrims to be treasured in more than a routine way. I have come to believe that here is a leadership content and style which, deep down, we know America — and our congregation — must have.

Here is a nuclear model for continuing education in ministry. Ideally this exposition which I now make — and conversation upon it — should be preceded by a corporate celebration by a congregation of the whole Pilgrim enterprise. For then the living content would already be interiorized, and all would have something with which to discuss. As you will see in reading it, this paper was written for such an occasion. I think such a combination of events is an important invention for the life of a congregation and a pastor's effectiveness in communication.

One other introduction is necessary. I am using the word "multiplet" as a name for that type of organism which these four Pilgrim men were. I am using the word as a metaphor from the field of physics, in order to talk about an event and actuality in the realm of ecology of spirit.

A multiplet is a family of energies that — as they become "a family" of energies — speed each other up to the speed of light. They have that effect on each other.

And the thrusts are no longer random, but orbit together. Arranged in architectonic structure, they not only mount up intense power, but mutually reinforce each other from the inside. Now no one energy can be collapsed, bumped off course, attacked into destruction. Reinforcing energies flow in, the **entire structure** refuses to collapse, to be de-natured. No longer is each a vanishing blip on a couldn't-care-less screen, but an infra-structure.

Only a human society can adequately be this kind of multiplet. For human beings can interiorize each other and the whole together. So that the multiplet is not only "out there," but also resides in the innerness of each person within it. What help do we get if we use this multiplet model to explore the leadership we are looking for and planning to develop?

THE PILGRIM MULTIPLET

We have just re-lived in celebration what the Pilgrim was all about. We should not leave them without identifying what may be learned about leadership of religious enterprise. My first hunch is — leadership must be a corporate phenomenon. The second hypothesis is this: in these four men, taken together, we have a model of corporate leadership. In them we have a full orb of powers necessary for something important to happen. We have answers to the questions: What is the substance of "potent, desirable minister?" What is a congregation's armament for Christian enterprise? Each of these four men — and all of them together — can be memorable symbols of religious functioning which vitalizes a congregation. So now to examine each man, and name his distinctive content of leadership.

1

Bradford is the able planner and leader of total enterprises. The people understand what their common enterprise is about, because they understand him.

He is the Significant Other, dwelling in the heart-mind of all members of the congregation. So that they are a **communal** society. He is the central person whom all understand in about the same way — and they all know that they do. He is somewhat dependably a power within all for congruent action. And they all know that this is so.

Bradford is also a symbol of the Generalized Other. That is, of the enterprise of history-making that they are all part of, and of the plot of life which together they are living out. From time to time they experience consummatory peaks of that drama.

Further he excels in interpreting rightful possibilities in the situations that arise — quite practically and concretely. Partly because he is consultative wisdom. Partly because over a period of originative years he has put together a story of their enterprise "setting out thru time toward a destiny," and successfully brought that developing story to bear on numerous decisions. Unknown to many, he also is weaving together his interpretation of that history story and putting it into a book. So that not only his contemporaries, but generations to come can feel its fascination as a statement of human possibility. He is trying to discern the working of the hand of God in their history.

Bradford is not afraid to use power, yet does not do so to serve individualistic advantage. He excels in governance of active peers who intend aboundingness of life. Who rejoice in their mutual claims upon each other and the good of all. It is felt that, at his best, he utters the "speaking words" of the Holy Spirit present in their corporateness, the speaking words of the future that is not yet but even now present in their midst, the speaking words of the God of the Bible. Not he alone, but also the communal tradition and the experiencing of the congregation are forming his decisions. He is a "man of action." And not merely in terms of custom, but of a continuity of meanings-to-live.

2

Elder Brewster is the teacher of the congregation and community, the developer of the person as religious consciousness.

He explicates — as one who is contemporary with events and lived experience — a total vision of life (the Bible). He communicates world image, not this and that opinion.

He is steeped in the New Learning — i.e., not technical knowhow, but humanness. The life of the mind is a religious phenomenon. (Cambridge was a most exciting place in his University days.)

He equips his people with tools for culturing their lived moments . . . with a system of language which forms them. They become able to transform fate into destiny, earth into world. They have a distinctive and considered life style.

As he teaches, they check him out. For they themselves have experiences and voice and access to the originating documents.

He is further determined that the people of his time have access to controversial documents dealing with current life-death issues. In Leyden he runs a Pilgrim Press in the attic of his own home, so that information and hot brains can pour out into the arena of public opinion forming. He is mass communication in his time.

He is the "teacher who has been there." He himself has participated in public life, experienced the ways of diplomacy and how to fight for freedom-loving people. He is wisdom — the maturing of a keen mind during a lifetime. He opens his own home as a nesting place for singing unto the Lord a new song.

He teaches his people how to teach their own inwardness to be in charge of its development and purification. He excels in publicly laying open the heart to God. They begin to understand their inner-personal region, and establish there inward truth work. He is an expert in interiority, as well as a man of deeds!

He is a multi-dimensional teacher.

3

And what is the mode of religious leadership that we might label "John Robinson?"

Robinson is the ordained pastor, graduate of a University where over a period of years a new learning is developing. This learning, and the people sent out from the school, fuels and guides the emerging battle for each person's right to be person. Likewise the emerging battle that dominion be wrested from the existing "imperial presidencies," untouchable ecclesiastics, church members who no longer "believe in." For these three are a pollution, a numbness of choking off possibility of vitality and meaning.

Robinson and his gathered congregation found each other because both were walking in a way of the Lord in their own time on earth. So they discovered each other. And the walk was not "this is the way I feel," "this is how I actualize my potential and feed my need", but a participation in the working of God's hand in civilization making. Once more light was being brought forth in a wilderness determined to remain dark.

Robinson was pastor of the Scrooby-Leyden congregation for twelve years, and in those years the Pilgrims were formed. A "spirit formation" took place which enabled them as a church and settlement to go on their own. They were without ordained pastor their first nine years in America, they succeeded as laymen. And they got the best of any later pastor who tried to trivialize the Pilgrim walk and reduce it to custom.

There is no adequate word for such a pastor, no adequate metaphor. Robinson was not just about "the care and cure of souls" — as if his congregation was blobs of sickness and fragile non-entities. Rather they were, in his eyes, hard-hitting exemplars of that which was going to be. He was not a leader of conferences on death and dying — his people were not interested in the death of the personal, but in its birthing. He was about bringing off a congregation, a civilization. His congregation was realistic in the Bonhoeffer sense. They were journeying in a world created, loved, judged, transformed by God. In that "worlding" was their existence. They were not "merrie England" committed to a life of sensation, consumerism, Merry Mount unfaithfulness. They imaged themselves as God's free people. They were determined to be **citizens** of their church and nation. They became tenacity in the face of adversity.

Robinson and his people had a basic document whose history and teaching they were expounding. They had Torah in their hands and in their heart. In the world, there was a Sacred that could not be profaned with impunity, or its structures violated for long. They had lived long enough in the events of their time to know that a mere pluralism reduced a nation to impotence and a church to a Sargasso Sea. They had a Constitution, a Bill of Rights, a Scripture, a tradition to be purified and developed, a God whom to serve was freedom, generative events to be expressed in their day.

For they had been taught by their pastor and invited to teach. They taught each other in common searchings for what to live by. So they were self-propelling.

They understood a common convictional language. They believed that Good was meant to have dominion. The times, themselves, and Pastor Robinson brought about in them the broad ethic of a justice culture, a democracy of moral plenteousness.

"The Spirit flames, and words of truth are spoken with
great power"
"But take heed that what you receive is Truth."

4

Every religious enterprise requires appreciative consciousness. And expressive power and forms that everyone can join in.

As Henry Ainsworth read the Psalms in Hebrew, he felt a grace in the language itself that required a ten syllable line in English to faithfully present the melody of its thought. Then he sought Dutch and French tunes — arising out of the singing of the people through the years — that had the same grace and melody.

But most importantly, he felt that humankind's sensitive, appreciative dialogue with God was present in the Psalms in a way that made them Scripture for him and the English people. So he first translated the Psalms into English prose, then re-formed the expression into metrical rhythm, with the lines answering each other thru the rhyming of their last words.

And the Psalms are meant to be **sung**! And publicly — so that the singer is making a statement. The Psalms are to be sung **corporately** — for so the congregation has immediate taste of the heavenly existence to which they are called. The human voice (particularly when singing with full voice, and understanding what it is singing) is not a mere maker of sound, but an act of the Holy Spirit itself forming the words, and tuning them into "spirit congregated." For the Pilgrim, the human voice which we all are, was the most sacred music that could be produced on earth. No matter how attractive lutes and bass viols were as embellishment, **human singing uttering words** was in a class by itself. Meaningful art was uttered by the Sacred!

With Ainsworth's Psalter (1611) in their hands and heart, the Pilgrims had their own indigenous religious art form. It was themselves, yet tied them into the church universal and all humankind. For the book of Psalms (and indeed Hebrew poetry) is mind searching to understand and live toward human destiny.

Ainsworth's Psalmody was the phenomenologizing — not only of the Hebrew, but of the Pilgrims. With it, they could corporately make sense out of their experiences, and dwell in God. Restore a sense of the sacred as a component of their world.

In his translation Ainsworth was exuberant. "Shout to Jehovah, all the earth . . . come before his presence with singing mirth."

Appreciative consciousness . . .
  Artistic consciousness . . .
    Hungry for meanings consciousness . . .
      Tragic consciousness . . .
        Delighting in consummations and beautiful form consciousness . . .
        Voicing "I believe" together.

The Ainsworth function is that of instigator-enabler of communal celebration by A People. Those who enable their people to keep centering down, and to re-mean their center. To treasure the things that matter most, and re-light their memories. Ainsworth tried to make sure that the people understood "the root of the matter," and so annotated his translation of each Psalm, opening up lines of interpretation so that the vibrations of the singers' minds would be as the strumming of an organum.

With Ainsworth, the Pilgrims built up a richness of inner speech . . . expressed in first-order language. And they uttered it publicly and before themselves, without apology.

The inventive congregational music and singing of our time is probably coming from "block" congregations — both Protestant and Catholic. So they may become "Ainsworth" to us all. The tunes and lyrics the established white churches sing are pretty confined to the eighteenth and nineteenth centuries.

We have run out of something significant to say in Significant Form? We are scared to use the multi-languages now available to symbolize and communicate what matters most? The restoration of congregational singing in the Pilgrim style awaits the nod of sleepy worship commissions? We want to be sung to, rather than universally sing? We are addicted to electronic art -- which is pseudo-personal? We know not how to use the local artists.

But beginnings are about to break out. The day of the laymen and the artist in celebrative worship may be at hand.

A LEADERSHIP SYSTEM

These four persons were a leadership **multiplet** . . . a **family of energies** that moved each other up to the speed of light. And there **was** light.

So we have a model of corporate leadership. It is such a team as the Pilgrim multiplet. The description of these men which we have presented — both in the celebration and in this analysis — is a vision of the **essential** of **pastor**, the essential of **teacher**, the essential of **enterprise leader**, the essential of **appreciative celebrator**. But what happens when you put these all together? Either in one person, or four persons, or as "departments of functioning" by a congregation?

However it is done (and probably all modes are necessary), we now have a model of "leadings on" which a pastor and a congregation must be. If we go the corporate route, many members will be enlisted for excellence in these leadings. Knowing that all of these functionings are necessary if there is to be growth of spirit, if congregation enterprise is to come about, if something more than a laissez-faire conglomerate will be the fate of their church.

My hypothesis is that only with such an orb of leadings on can a congregation arrive . . . a group of people who believe in something together, and in each other. And so themselves become a Pilgrim multiplet.

Development religiously is a corporateness of these functionings. These four are a **system** of religious growth.

TOGETHER BELIEVING IN SOMETHING

But there is another major learning for us from the Pilgrim multiplet. Perhaps it is a quality-content that made it a multiplet, and not a conglomerate.

The Pilgrim multiplet **believed in** each other. And together they **believed in** a reality world within which they enterprised.

They believed in each other. They understood each other and they all knew that they did. Ainsworth, Robinson, Brewster, Bradford — each and together — had a dependable picture of each other's inner citadel revealed through years of tough going. They had respectfully interiorized each other; they indwelt each other as a power of making worlds. Together they were an ethos, a distinctive character structure, a life biography with intense themes and episodes, rite of passage from nebulous mass man. They spoke a common web of inner speech. They affirmed that they were a style of Christian Existence. They had a troth from which they could not be pushed, and from which all other choices developed.

But equally important, together they believed in (William James' meaning of "belief") a certain reality world. They believed in a meaning-fulized, interpreted earth, and so had a high sense of participating in

142

reality. Reality as defined in the Bonhoeffer sense. Reality as the world as being created, loved, judged, re-meaned and re-deeded by a God present in humankind's venture, taking form in a band of persons.

So they understood the large enterprise they were about in about the same way. Even though they might start with different opinions about what ought to be done in a particular situation and how it could be brought off.

They were a system of Significant Symbols.

"Worlding," to them, was a religious enterprise.

The Pilgrim multiplet had the learning which possessed the Calvinist — the learning that there is a Sacred that cannot be profaned or trivialized with impunity. The learning that Reality is earth being created, loved, judged, transformed into possibility fit for **human** beings, by a God terrible in his concern for a justice culture. A God who is ahead of his people on a destiny journey in this wilderness world. And who is not just "out there," but at the same time is an inexhaustible fountain-head out of which strength and originatings flow.

The other learning of a Calvinist was vocation. To serve the God of this reality world is perfect freedom. To be about building, loving, judging, transforming a world of some size we can be particularly responsible in. Vocation living is not identical with ministry as of the Scribes and Pharisees, for the emphasis and invitation is upon **being**, upon participation in the enterprising.

Such a vocation calls into being "The Lord's Free People" who individually and congregationally are citizens of a history-making both of a church and of a nation's culture.

For "vocation" means "covenant", which means "to walk together", which means "connected with each other's good and the source of all good." To become individuated, but not individualistic. To achieve stubborn and principled integrity within some continuing stream of the species humankind.

Being a Pilgrim multiplet means being held together by some forming tradition . . . not of custom, but of a zeal for truth-being.

God . . . vocation . . . covenant . . . principled individuation . . . "I believe in" as the source and sustainer of "I AM" . . . these are key meanings that make possible a multiplet religious leadership.

Religious leadership of this style of multiplet has exciting conversation ahead of it with two current developments in the world of learning. Namely psychohistory and historymyth. Erikson, Coles, Lifton, are now developing a psychology no longer limited to conditioning theory, brainwashing, Oedipus complex, therapies that ignore person as expressive identity, constitutor of destiny, participant in great surges of human spirit, shaper of symbol formations and a culture of meanings which he sometimes prizes above life itself.

Psychohistory is opening up the study of persons who in their own "living a **life**" also struggle with the crucial development which has to be brought off in the history-making of their time. Current studies are also discovering that always some persons have lived in most disastrous social events, and still were not reduced from being a human dignity, nor dry-cleaned of spirit. Though terribly hurt, they were not destroyed.

Possibly we all now instinctively feel that maybe we better be about discovering how such is possible. How is it possible that we can be "afflicted in every way, but not crushed; perplexed but not driven to despair; persecuted, but not forsaken; struck down but not destroyed?" How also can we mutter thru clenched teeth: "Come down, O daughter (and sons) of Babylon. Come down, sit in the dust. There is no throne!"

The secret of a life that overcomes the actual, has something to do with mythhistory . . . an interpretation of human event not confined to actuality but transcending it, not encaved in one moment but weaving together many moments. And so proclaims a potency still struggling to become real . . . in us.

Entertain the possibility that the Pilgrim multiplet is one such worthy psychohistory and mythhistory. And do not worry that the little town of Plymouth didn't become capitol of the United States. Accept it as a culture gift.

TIMING WITH CULTURING NOW GOING ON IN OUR COUNTRY

As we work to keep alive a healthy civil religion in a pluralistic society, the religious actuality of the Pilgrims is especially significant. For, unlike New England, they were depth minded enough to know that even they had not yet "bottomed out" all of God's truth. And they were not warped by a "manifest destiny" to have dominion over church and state . . . as some New England divines sometimes seemed to be.

But, on the other hand, they were not apologetic or numb about the light that did come through to them. They were determined that the State should never have absolute dominion over all life — a determination greatly to be treasured in an era of one man imperialisms, government by totalistic propaganda and controls. They were against any form of a state church which had dominion over religious culture . . . even an indigenous bureaucracy attempting to lead toward the time when on a given Sunday every congregation will use the same order of worship, recite the same prayers, be preached to on the same verses from a pericope, using the same throw-away notes published on the Bible passage by a unitary religious press, ministers wearing the same pretty vestments, isolated at the same spot in a designated church year.

The Pilgrim style of Christian life and works is significantly relevant to what Richard Neuhaus titles "American Dream, Churches Agenda." For — to alter slightly the title of his book — many people feel that this is a "time toward homing," i.e., a time to help form a religious home for a pluralistic society . . . Something more than individualistic valuings, sensation and impulses and orgasm, ethnic purity and saga, electronic culture. There's at least a psychohistory we are weaving together, a world reality we know we participate in, an ecology of spirit which, from time to time, breaks out in power. Perhaps the experiment of America is revelation!

Not more religious gadgetry, but numinous power is the rightful seeking of this generation.

BIBLIOGRAPHY

Bartlett, Robert Merrill, *The Pilgrim Way* (Philadelphia: United Church Press, 1971).

Bradford, William, *Of Plymouth Plantation,* edited by S. E. Morrison (New York: Alfred Knopf, 1952).

Pratt, Waldo Selden, *The Music of the Pilgrims* (Boston: Oliver Ditson, 1922).

Smith, Bradford, *Bradford of Plymouth* (Philadelphia: Lippincott, 1951).